Edited by Willi

EDWIN MURRAY

SELECTED

POEMS

OF

Robert Browning

Appleton-Century-Crofts, Inc.

NEW YORK

Contents

Introduction

LIKE most men of letters who deal seriously with men and women and the moral and religious problems which they face in life, Robert Browning was slow in finding his most characteristic and effective mode of expression. It should be said, however, that part of his tardiness in coming into his own, as well as much of the flavor of his subjects and his treatment of them, was owing to his almost total lack of formal education. The son and grandson of officials in the banking institutions of London, Robert Browning was educated mainly at home in Camberwell in his father's substantial but casually chosen library. His parents seem to have been indulgent to all the desires of the young genius of the family. He was permitted to forego his formal schooling while still a boy, and under the guidance of an occasional tutor in Italian, French, and music he read voraciously, and visited the picture galleries across the green fields at Dulwich. Thus the young man grew to maturity with his mind multitudinously stocked with an amateur's knowledge of music, painting, history, and literature, especially Greek and English. In this condition, Browning at twenty was entirely confident that he could be a poet, a novelist, a painter, a writer of operas, or perhaps even a statesman, all at once.

It was probably his youthful discovery of Shelley and Keats which determined Browning's career, and the marks of his discipleship to Shelley lingered in his poetry for many years. In the long process of finding his own voice Browning went through two major phases. In the first he wrote long poems of a "confessional" nature—*Pauline* (1833), *Paracelsus* (1835), and *Sordello* (1840)—in which his conception of poetry, as we can see through all his disguises, is a notion that the poet looked in his heart and wrote, that the perfect bard was one who "shadowed forth the stages of all life." In this he obviously meant the inner life of the poet himself, and these poems are thinly disguised biography in which the poet through imaginary characters canvasses the poetic, moral, and religious problems which are troubling him at the time.

In writing this kind of poetry Browning was in a main

literary stream of his time. Autobiographical literature, sometimes in the guise of the life-drama or the moral confession, and sometimes as a frank exploitation of personality, came to nineteenth-century England from two main sources: the native source of moral confession stemmed from such Puritan writers as Bunyan and Baxter; the Continental source of personal and esthetic confessions, often merely a delight in the oddities and intricacies of one's own nature, came most directly from Rousseau. The native moral and the Continental esthetic confessions mingle strangely in such poems as Wordsworth's "Prelude," Coleridge's "Ode to Dejection," Byron's "Childe Harold" and "Don Juan," and much of Shelley's verse, and in such prose works as Lamb's *Essays,* DeQuincey's *Opium-Eater,* and Carlyle's *Sartor Resartus.* This literature did not die with the Romantic generation, but lasted into the Victorian, and nowhere is there a more odd blending of moral and esthetic confession than is to be found in Browning's three long poems of this kind. But for all its fine passages, *Pauline* did not sell a copy. The little volume was sharply but privately reviewed by John Stuart Mill. In the poem Browning had worn his heart openly upon his sleeve, and after Mill's rough treatment, he resolved never to do so again. *Paracelsus,* appearing in 1835, was a life-drama in five acts, but behind the thin disguise of dramatic characters, Browning was still writing confessional verse. *Sordello,* which he toiled over for seven years, was also disguised autobiography and much longer. All the doubts, fears, hopes, aspirations, failures, and renewed aspirations of the poet are told at length, but cloudily and under masks of various sorts. The poem was an abject failure, and with its appearance in 1840 Browning abandoned the long confessional poem. Nevertheless, the writing of such poems had taught him much of the inner operations of the spirit.

The relative success of *Paracelsus* brought the young poet into the brilliant world of the theatrical people of London, and under the influence of Macready, the tragedian, he produced his first play, *Strafford,* in 1837. It was an interesting subject, but not a good play, and ran only for four nights. Thereafter, for almost ten years Browning thought of himself as a writer of plays, and published a long series of them: *King Victor and King Charles* (1842); *A Blot in the 'Scutcheon* (1843); *The Return of the Druses* (1843); *Colombe's Birthday* (1844); and *Luria* and *A Soul's Tragedy*

(1846). None of these was successful on the stage. *A Blot*, the *Druses* and *Luria* are modelled upon Shakespeare and are touched by the melodramatic effects of Bulwer-Lytton, the most successful playwright of the 1840s. It is easily seen that in the formal drama, written to be acted on the boards, Browning had not found his proper voice. The reasons for this are several: Browning's habit of elaborate self-analysis by his characters was not suited to the action demanded upon the stage; Browning's subjects for the most part were remote from the interests and knowledge of his audience; lastly, Browning's mode of expression was intensely personal, and he had little of the dramatist's ability to fit his ideas and his language to a number of characters within a play. For these among other reasons Browning failed as a playwright for the Victorian stage, but in the process of writing plays he learned techniques of dramatic presentation which were to prove of inestimable value to him in his career as a poet.

As one may see at a glance, the first two phases of Browning's career overlapped each other, since he had begun to write plays while he was still engaged in finishing *Sordello*. The overlapping is likewise characteristic of the third phase of Browning's career, in which we see the poet coming slowly to an ever clearer conception of the nature of the dramatic monologue, the form of poetry which he was to make his own. In this form he was able to combine the soul-searching analyses of the confessional poem with the sharp dramatic situation. In a moment of crisis or decision the single character speaks his mind and heart, and often discloses more of himself than he knows.

The discovery of this form of poetry as best suited to his genius did not come all at once. As early as 1836 Browning had published a short poem, "Porphyria's Lover," which we may now see as his first step towards the dramatic monologue. But in that poem the poet, obviously more interested in the strange event than in the character of the speaker, retained the rhymed couplets better suited to narrative poetry. In the *Dramatic Lyrics* of 1842 Browning took a long stride towards his goal. In such poems as "Count Gismond," "Incident of the French Camp," and even the "Soliloquy of the Spanish Cloister," the poet is still more interested in story, atmosphere, and situation than he is in the portrayal of character, and the rhymed form of the verse illustrates his interest. But in one poem in that volume Browning almost achieved a perfect dramatic monologue, in the poem that came to be known as "My Last Duchess." There is some evidence to show that this poem was a happy accident. Browning's major interest at this time was almost certainly in the hard plight of the Duchess, and the poem began in the poet's mind as an illustration of the pitiful lot of a young, sensitive girl in the cold and ruthless power of an Italian nobleman of the sixteenth century. But the poet's habit of dramatic expression came to his aid; the story is put into the mouth of the Duke himself, and almost imperceptibly the Duke becomes the character of primary interest. Here Browning attains the essential method of the dramatic monologue, and only the faintly rhyming couplets of the verse, and perhaps the title of the poem itself, remain to remind us that the poet in 1842 possibly did not quite realize what he had done.

In the pamphlet of poems published in 1845 and called *Dramatic Romances and Lyrics* Browning made the final step, in the poem which came to be known as "The Bishop Orders his Tomb at Saint Praxed's Church." Here we have all the true elements of the dramatic monologue—the situation in the dying bishop, the shadowy audience in his sons, the profound revelation by the speaker of his innermost nature, and finally the compact blank verse that answers so readily to the mood of the speaker and is free from the necessities and shackles of rhyme. But in the *Dramatic Romances and Lyrics*, "The Bishop Orders his Tomb" is almost alone in this excellence, and there is obvious evidence that even in this poem Browning was quite as much interested in illustrating the corruption of Renaissance Italy as he was in the peculiar character of the bishop. In the slower pace of life in Italy after his marriage Browning began to see the clear line of his own development, and saw also what he could do that no other poet had done so well. We get the result of his contemplation in the two superb volumes of 1855, *Men and Women,* in such full-bodied dramatic monologues as "Fra Lippo Lippi," "Karshish," "Blougram," "Andrea del Sarto," and "Cleon." From that point, Browning went on in later years to produce the tremendous collection of dramatic monologues upon a single story which he called *The Ring and the Book.* Before he began to write the poem he conceived of it as his *magnum opus,* and it was inevitable that the matter should have been presented in a series of dramatic monologues, a form of poetry upon which he had put his own indelible stamp. It was a form of poetry which was to be exploited extensively by the poets of the twentieth century.

The dramatic monologue was, of course, not the only poetic form in which Browning triumphed. In the *Dramatic Lyrics* and the *Dramatic Romances and Lyrics* of 1842 he had begun to write short poems, often lyrical, which afforded sudden new and sharp insights into the hearts of men and women. The pair of little poems called "Meeting at Night" and "Parting at Morning" will serve admirably as an illustration of this kind of poetry. In *Men and Women* of 1855 the whole anatomy of love between men and women is laid bare as it had not been since John Donne ceased to write. One need only mention a few such poems as "Love Among the Ruins," "A Lovers' Quarrel," "A Woman's Last Word," "Any Wife to Any Husband," "The Statue and the Bust," "The Last Ride Together," "Two in the Campagna," "By the Fireside," and the intensely personal poem, "One Word More," in which he dedicated the volumes to his wife.

As he grew older a more serious consideration of moral and religious questions tended to take precedence over the creation of character and the sharp psychological insights of his middle years. This tendency had appeared in such relatively early poems as "Saul," "Cleon," and "Karshish," and is the chief element in such later triumphs as "Abt Vogler," "Rabbi Ben Ezra," and "Caliban," published in *Dramatis Personae* in 1864, three years after the death of his wife. The poet continued to write for twenty-five years after this date, and he continued to produce dramatic monologues for twenty years after *The Ring and the Book* of 1868-69, but not many memorable characters were created, as his poetry turned more and more to argument. By 1870 his significant contribution to English poetry was mainly made, and while there are a few poems of the later years which we would not willingly miss, the great task was done. Save for the mountainous achievement of *The Ring and the Book,* Browning's gift to English literature is fairly illustrated by the short poems, such as may be found in this volume.

Principal Dates in Browning's Life

1812   (May 7) Birth of Robert Browning at Camberwell, a suburb of London.

1833   *Pauline*, Browning's first poem.

1834   Journey to St. Petersburg, Russia.

1835   *Paracelsus*.

1837   Presentation of *Strafford*, Browning's first play, at Covent Garden.

1838   Browning's first Italian journey.

1840   *Sordello*.

1842   *Dramatic Lyrics*.

1843   *The Return of the Druses*.

1843   *A Blot in the 'Scutcheon*.

1844   Browning's second Italian journey.

1845   *Dramatic Romances and Lyrics*

1846   (September 12) Marriage of Browning to Elizabeth Barrett at St. Marylebone Church, and subsequent removal to Italy.

1849   Birth of a son, Robert Wiedemann Barrett Browning.

1855   *Men and Women*.

1861   Death of Mrs. Browning in Florence, and Browning's subsequent return to London.

1864   *Dramatis Personae*.

1868-9   *The Ring and the Book* in four volumes, issued monthly.

1881   Establishment of the Browning Society in London.

1889   (December 12) Death of Robert Browning in Venice. Burial in the Poet's Corner, Westminster Abbey.

Selected Poems of
ROBERT BROWNING

Song from "Pippa Passes"

THE year 's at the spring
And day 's at the morn;
Morning 's at seven;
The hillside 's dew-pearled;
The lark 's on the wing;
The snail 's on the thorn:
God 's in his heaven—
All 's right with the world!

My Last Duchess

FERRARA

Italian

THAT 's my last Duchess painted on the wall,
Looking as if she were alive. I call
That piece a wonder, now: Frà Pandolf's hands
Worked busily a day, and there she stands.
Will 't please you sit and look at her? I said
"Frà Pandolf" by design, for never read
Strangers like you that pictured countenance,
The depth and passion of its earnest glance,
But to myself they turned (since none puts by
The curtain I have drawn for you, but I)   10
And seemed as they would ask me, if they durst,
How such a glance came there; so, not the first
Are you to turn and ask thus. Sir, 't was not
Her husband's presence only, called that spot
Of joy into the Duchess' cheek: perhaps
Frà Pandolf chanced to say "Her mantle laps
"Over my lady's wrist too much," or "Paint

3 **Frà Pandolf** an imaginary painter

1

"Must never hope to reproduce the faint
"Half-flush that dies along her throat": such stuff
20 Was courtesy, she thought, and cause enough
For calling up that spot of joy. She had
A heart—how shall I say?—too soon made glad,
Too easily impressed; she liked whate'er
She looked on, and her looks went everywhere.
Sir, 't was all one! My favor at her breast,
The dropping of the daylight in the West,
The bough of cherries some officious fool
Broke in the orchard for her, the white mule
She rode with round the terrace—all and each
30 Would draw from her alike the approving speech,
Or blush, at least. She thanked men,—good! but thanked
Somehow—I know not how—as if she ranked
My gift of a nine-hundred-years-old name
With anybody's gift. Who 'd stoop to blame
This sort of trifling? Even had you skill
In speech—(which I have not)—to make your will
Quite clear to such an one, and say, "Just this
"Or that in you disgusts me; here you miss,
"Or there exceed the mark"—and if she let
40 Herself be lessoned so, nor plainly set
Her wits to yours, forsooth, and made excuse,
—E'en then would be some stooping; and I choose
Never to stoop. Oh sir, she smiled, no doubt,
Whene'er I passed her; but who passed without
Much the same smile? This grew; I gave commands;
Then all smiles stopped together. There she stands
As if alive. Will 't please you rise? We 'll meet   'get up'
The company below, then. I repeat,
The Count your master's known munificence
50 Is ample warrant that no just pretense
Of mine for dowry will be disallowed;
Though his fair daughter's self, as I avowed
At starting, is my object. Nay, we 'll go
Together down, sir. Notice Neptune, though,
Taming a sea horse, thought a rarity,
Which Claus of Innsbruck cast in bronze for me!

56 **Claus of Innsbruck** an imaginary artist

Count Gismond

AIX IN PROVENCE

I

CHRIST God who savest man, save most
  Of men Count Gismond who saved me!
Count Gauthier, when he chose his post,
  Chose time and place and company
To suit it; when he struck at length
My honor, 't was with all his strength.

II

And doubtlessly ere he could draw
  All points to one, he must have schemed!
That miserable morning saw
  Few half so happy as I seemed,   10
While being dressed in queen's array
To give our tourney prize away.

III

I thought they loved me, did me grace
  To please themselves; 't was all their deed;
God makes, or fair or foul, our face;
  If showing mine so caused to bleed
My cousins' hearts, they should have dropped
A word, and straight the play had stopped.

IV

They, too, so beauteous! Each a queen
  By virtue of her brow and breast;   20
Not needing to be crowned, I mean,
  As I do. E'en when I was dressed,
Had either of them spoke, instead
Of glancing sideways with still head!

V

But no: they let me laugh, and sing
  My birthday song quite through, adjust
The last rose in my garland, fling
  A last look on the mirror, trust

My arms to each an arm of theirs,
30 And so descend the castle-stairs—

VI

And come out on the morning-troop
    Of merry friends who kissed my cheek,
And called me queen, and made me stoop
    Under the canopy—(a streak
That pierced it, of the outside sun,
Powdered with gold its gloom's soft dun)—

VII

And they could let me take my state
    And foolish throne amid applause
Of all come there to celebrate
40   My queen's-day—Oh I think the cause
Of much was, they forgot no crowd
Makes up for parents in their shroud!

VIII

However that be, all eyes were bent
    Upon me, when my cousins cast
Theirs down; 't was time I should present
    The victor's crown, but . . . there, 't will last
No long time . . . the old mist again
Blinds me as then it did. How vain!

IX

See! Gismond 's at the gate, in talk
50   With his two boys: I can proceed.
Well, at that moment, who should stalk
    Forth boldly—to my face, indeed—
But Gauthier, and he thundered "Stay!"
And all stayed. "Bring no crowns, I say!

X

"Bring torches! Wind the penance-sheet
    "About her! Let her shun the chaste,
"Or lay herself before their feet!
    "Shall she whose body I embraced
"A night long, queen it in the day?
60 "For honor's sake no crowns, I say!"

XI

I? What I answered? As I live,
　I never fancied such a thing
As answer possible to give.
　What says the body when they spring
Some monstrous torture-engine's whole
Strength on it? No more says the soul.

XII

Till out strode Gismond; then I knew
　That I was saved. I never met
His face before, but, at first view,
　I felt quite sure that God had set   70
Himself to Satan; who would spend
A minute's mistrust on the end?

XIII

He strode to Gauthier, in his throat
　Gave him the lie, then struck his mouth
With one backhanded blow that wrote
　In blood men's verdict there. North, South,
East, West, I looked. The lie was dead,
And damned, and truth stood up instead.

XIV

This glads me most, that I enjoyed
　The heart of the joy, with my content   80
In watching Gismond unalloyed
　By any doubt of the event:
God took that on him—I was bid
Watch Gismond for my part: I did.

XV

Did I not watch him while he let
　His armorer just brace his greaves,
Rivet his hauberk, on the fret
　The while! His foot . . . my memory leaves
No least stamp out, nor how anon
He pulled his ringing gauntlets on.   90

XVI

And e'en before the trumpet's sound
　Was finished, prone lay the false knight,

Prone as his lie, upon the ground:
　　Gismond flew at him, used no sleight
O' the sword, but open-breasted drove,
Cleaving till out the truth he clove.

XVII

Which done, he dragged him to my feet
　　And said "Here die, but end thy breath
"In full confession, lest thou fleet
　　"From my first, to God's second death!
"Say, hast thou lied?" And, "I have lied
"To God and her," he said, and died.

XVIII

Then Gismond, kneeling to me, asked
　　—What safe my heart holds, though no word
Could I repeat now, if I tasked
　　My powers forever, to a third
Dear even as you are. Pass the rest
Until I sank upon his breast.

XIX

Over my head his arm he flung
　　Against the world; and scarce I felt
His sword (that dripped by me and swung)
　　A little shifted in its belt.
For he began to say the while
How South our home lay many a mile.

XX

So 'mid the shouting multitude
　　We two walked forth to never more
Return. My cousins have pursued
　　Their life, untroubled as before
I vexed them. Gauthier's dwelling-place
God lighten! May his soul find grace!

XXI

Our elder boy has got the clear
　　Great brow; tho' when his brother's black

Full eye shows scorn, it . . . Gismond here?
   And have you brought my tercel back?
I just was telling Adela
How many birds it struck since May.

Incident of the French Camp

I

You know, we French stormed Ratisbon:
   A mile or so away,
On a little mound, Napoleon
   Stood on our storming-day;
With neck outthrust, you fancy how,
   Legs wide, arms locked behind,
As if to balance the prone brow
   Oppressive with its mind.

II

Just as perhaps he mused "My plans
   "That soar, to earth may fall,   10
"Let once my army leader Lannes
   "Waver at yonder wall,"—
Out 'twixt the battery-smokes there flew
   A rider, bound on bound
Full-galloping; nor bridle drew
   Until he reached the mound.

III

Then off there flung in smiling joy,
   And held himself erect
By just his horse's mane, a boy:
   You hardly could suspect—   20
(So tight he kept his lips compressed,
   Scarce any blood came through)
You looked twice ere you saw his breast
   Was all but shot in two.

124 **tercel** a male hawk, used in falconry   1 **Ratisbon** Regensburg in Bavaria, stormed by the French under Marshal Lannes on April 22, 1809

IV

"Well," cried he, "Emperor, by God's grace
   "We 've got you Ratisbon!
"The Marshal 's in the market place,
   "And you 'll be there anon
"To see your flag-bird flap his vans
30   "Where I, to heart's desire,
"Perched him!" The chief's eye flashed; his plans
   Soared up again like fire.

V

The chief's eye flashed; but presently
   Softened itself, as sheathes
A film the mother-eagle's eye
   When her bruised eaglet breathes;
"You 're wounded!" "Nay," the soldier's pride
   Touched to the quick, he said:
"I 'm killed, Sire!" And his chief beside
40   Smiling the boy fell dead.

Soliloquy of the Spanish Cloister

I

GR-R-R—there go, my heart's abhorrence!
   Water your damned flowerpots, do!
If hate killed men, Brother Lawrence,
   God's blood, would not mine kill you!
What? your myrtle bush wants trimming?
   Oh, that rose has prior claims—
Needs its leaden vase filled brimming?
   Hell dry you up with its flames!

II

At the meal we sit together:
10   *Salve tibi!* I must hear
Wise talk of the kind of weather,
   Sort of season, time of year:
Not a plenteous cork-crop: scarcely
   Dare we hope oak-galls, I doubt:

10 **Salve tibi** hail to you

What 's the Latin name for "parsley"?
What 's the Greek name for Swine's Snout?

III

Whew! We 'll have our platter burnished,
  Laid with care on our own shelf!
With a fire-new spoon we 're furnished,
  And a goblet for ourself,   20
Rinsed like something sacrificial
  Ere 't is fit to touch our chaps—
Marked with L. for our initial!
  (He-he! There his lily snaps!)

IV   *doubt & moral.*

Saint, forsooth! While brown Dolores
  Squats outside the Convent bank
With Sanchicha, telling stories,
  Steeping tresses in the tank,
Blue-black, lustrous, thick like horsehairs,
  —Can't I see his dead eye glow,   30
Bright as 't were a Barbary corsair's?
  (That is, if he 'd let it show!)

V

When he finishes refection,
  Knife and fork he never lays
Crosswise, to my recollection,
  As do I, in Jesu's praise.
I the Trinity illustrate,
  Drinking watered orange-pulp—
In three sips the Arian frustrate;
  While he drains his at one gulp.   40

VI

Oh, those melons? If he 's able
  We 're to have a feast! so nice!
One goes to the Abbot's table,
  All of us get each a slice.
How go on your flowers? None double?
  Not one fruit-sort can you spy?

31 **Barbary corsair** a pirate from the northern coast of Africa 39 **Arian**
a follower of Arius, who in the fourth century denied that Christ was
equal with God the Father

Strange!—And I, too, at such trouble,
    Keep them close-nipped on the sly!

VII

There 's a great text in Galatians,
50   Once you trip on it, entails   *dogma*
Twenty-nine distinct damnations,
    One sure, if another fails:
If I trip him just a-dying,
    Sure of heaven as sure can be,
Spin him round and send him flying
    Off to hell, a Manichee?

VIII

Or, my scrofulous French novel
    On grey paper with blunt type!
Simply glance at it, you grovel
60   Hand and foot in Belial's gripe:
If I double down its pages
    At the woeful sixteenth print,
When he gathers his greengages,   *plums*
    Ope a sieve and slip it in 't?

IX

Or, there 's Satan!—one might venture
    Pledge one's soul to him, yet leave
Such a flaw in the indenture
    As he 'd miss till, past retrieve,
Blasted lay that rose-acacia — *a plant*.
70   We 're so proud of! *Hy, Zy, Hine* . . .
'St, there 's Vespers! *Plena gratiâ
    Ave, Virgo!* Gr-r-r—you swine!

---

49 **Galatians** St. Paul's Epistle to the Galatians v:19-21   56 **Manichee** a
believer in the Manichean heresy, a doctrine which viewed the world as
an arena of conflict between good and evil, light and darkness 60 **Belial**
one of the devils 70 **Hy, Zy, Hine** perhaps the sound of the vesper bells,
but more probably the beginning of a curse against Lawrence 71 **Plena
gratiâ Ave, Virgo** Hail Mary, full of grace

Porphyria's Lover

THE rain set early in tonight,
   The sullen wind was soon awake,
It tore the elm-tops down for spite,
   And did its worst to vex the lake:
   I listened with heart fit to break.
When glided in Porphyria; straight
   She shut the cold out and the storm,
And kneeled and made the cheerless grate
   Blaze up, and all the cottage warm;
   Which done, she rose, and from her form   10
Withdrew the dripping cloak and shawl,
   And laid her soiled gloves by, untied
Her hat and let the damp hair fall,
   And, last, she sat down by my side
   And called me. When no voice replied,
She put my arm about her waist,
   And made her smooth white shoulder bare,
And all her yellow hair displaced,
   And, stooping, made my cheek lie there,
   And spread, o'er all, her yellow hair,   20
Murmuring how she loved me—she
   Too weak, for all her heart's endeavor,
To set its struggling passion free
   From pride, and vainer ties dissever,
   And give herself to me forever.
But passion sometimes would prevail,
   Nor could tonight's gay feast restrain
A sudden thought of one so pale
   For love of her, and all in vain:
   So, she was come through wind and rain.   30
Be sure I looked up at her eyes
   Happy and proud; at last I knew
Porphyria worshipped me; surprise
   Made my heart swell, and still it grew
   While I debated what to do.
That moment she was mine, mine, fair,
   Perfectly pure and good: I found

Title: This poem was written in Russia in 1834, and first published in 1842 as No. I. of *Madhouse Cells*

A thing to do, and all her hair
    In one long yellow string I wound
40   Three times her little throat around,
And strangled her. No pain felt she;
    I am quite sure she felt no pain.
As a shut bud that holds a bee,
    I warily oped her lids: again
    Laughed the blue eyes without a stain.
And I untightened next the tress
    About her neck; her cheek once more
Blushed bright beneath my burning kiss:
    I propped her head up as before,
50   Only, this time my shoulder bore
Her head, which droops upon it still:
    The smiling rosy little head,
So glad it has its utmost will,
    That all it scorned at once is fled,
    And I, its love, am gained instead!
Porphyria's love: she guessed not how
    Her darling one wish would be heard.
And thus we sit together now,
    And all night long we have not stirred,
60   And yet God has not said a word!

"How They Brought the Good News
From Ghent to Aix"

(16—)

I

I sprang to the stirrup, and Joris, and he;
I galloped, Dirck galloped, we galloped all three;
"Good speed!" cried the watch, as the gatebolts undrew;
"Speed!" echoed the wall to us galloping through;
Behind shut the postern, the lights sank to rest,
And into the midnight we galloped abreast.

Title: **Ghent** a city in Belgium about one hundred miles from Aix-la-Chapelle in Germany. Looz and Tongres lie out of the direct route and add twenty miles to the journey. 5 **postern** a back or side gate

II

Not a word to each other; we kept the great pace
Neck by neck, stride by stride, never changing our place;
I turned in my saddle and made its girths tight,
Then shortened each stirrup, and set the pique right,   10
Rebuckled the cheek-strap, chained slacker the bit,
Nor galloped less steadily Roland a whit.

III

'T was moonset at starting; but while we drew near
Lokeren, the cocks crew and twilight dawned clear;
At Boom, a great yellow star came out to see;
At Düffeld, 't was morning as plain as could be;
And from Mecheln church steeple we heard the half-chime,
So, Joris broke silence with, "Yet there is time!"

IV

At Aershot, up leaped of a sudden the sun,
And against him the cattle stood black every one,   20
To stare thro' the mist at us galloping past,
And I saw my stout galloper Roland at last,
With resolute shoulders, each butting away
The haze, as some bluff river headland its spray:

V

And his low head and crest, just one sharp ear bent back
For my voice, and the other pricked out on his track;
And one eye's black intelligence,—ever that glance
O'er its white edge at me, his own master, askance!
And the thick heavy spume-flakes which aye and anon
His fierce lips shook upwards in galloping on.   30

VI

By Hasselt, Dirck groaned; and cried Joris, "Stay spur!
"Your Roos galloped bravely, the fault 's not in her,
"We 'll remember at Aix"—for one heard the quick wheeze
Of her chest, saw the stretched neck and staggering knees,
And sunk tail, and horrible heave of the flank,
As down on her haunches she shuddered and sank.

10 **pique** pommel

VII

So, we were left galloping, Joris and I,
Past Looz and past Tongres, no cloud in the sky;
The broad sun above laughed a pitiless laugh,
40 'Neath our feet broke the brittle bright stubble like chaff;
Till over by Dalhem a dome-spire sprang white,
And "Gallop," gasped Joris, "for Aix is in sight!"

VIII

"How they 'll greet us!"—and all in a moment his roan
Rolled neck and croup over, lay dead as a stone;
And there was my Roland to bear the whole weight
Of the news which alone could save Aix from her fate,
With his nostrils like pits full of blood to the brim,
And with circles of red for his eye-sockets' rim.

IX

Then I cast loose my buffcoat, each holster let fall,
50 Shook off my jack-boots, let go belt and all,
Stood up in the stirrup, leaned, patted his ear,
Called my Roland his pet name, my horse without peer;
Clapped my hands, laughed and sang, any noise, bad or good,
Till at length into Aix Roland galloped and stood.

X

And all I remember is, friends flocking round
As I sat with his head 'twixt my knees on the ground;
And no voice but was praising this Roland of mine,
As I poured down his throat our last measure of wine,
Which (the burgesses voted by common consent)
60 Was no more than his due who brought good news from Ghent.

The Lost Leader

I

JUST for a handful of silver he left us,
    Just for a riband to stick in his coat—
Found the one gift of which fortune bereft us,
    Lost all the others she lets us devote;

Title: Browning admitted that this poem was a "fancy portrait of Wordsworth," who accepted a Civil List pension of £300 in 1842 ("a handful
of silver"), and the laureateship ("a riband to stick in his coat") in 1843

They, with the gold to give, doled him out silver,
   So much was theirs who so little allowed:
How all our copper had gone for his service!
   Rags—were they purple, his heart had been proud!
We that had loved him so, followed him, honored him,
   Lived in his mild and magnificent eye,   10
Learned his great language, caught his clear accents,
   Made him our pattern to live and to die!
Shakespeare was of us, Milton was for us,
Burns, Shelley, were with us,—they watch from their graves!
He alone breaks from the van and the freemen,
   —He alone sinks to the rear and the slaves!

II

We shall march prospering,—not thro' his presence;
   Songs may inspirit us,—not from his lyre;
Deeds will be done,—while he boasts his quiescence,
   Still bidding crouch whom the rest bade aspire: 20
Blot out his name, then, record one lost soul more,
   One task more declined, one more footpath untrod,
One more devils'-triumph and sorrow for angels,
   One wrong more to man, one more insult to God!
Life's night begins: let him never come back to us!
   There would be doubt, hesitation and pain,
Forced praise on our part—the glimmer of twilight,
   Never glad confident morning again!
Best fight on well, for we taught him—strike gallantly,
   Menace our heart ere we master his own;   30
Then let him receive the new knowledge and wait us,
   Pardoned in heaven, the first by the throne!

Home-Thoughts, from Abroad

I

   Oh, to be in England
   Now that April's there,
   And whoever wakes in England
   Sees, some morning, unaware,
   That the lowest boughs and the brushwood sheaf
   Round the elm-tree bole are in tiny leaf,

While the chaffinch sings on the orchard bough
In England—now!

II

And after April, when May follows,
10   And the whitethroat builds, and all the swallows!
Hark, where my blossomed pear tree in the hedge
Leans to the field and scatters on the clover
Blossoms and dewdrops—at the bent spray's edge—
That's the wise thrush; he sings each song twice over,
Lest you should think he never could recapture
The first fine careless rapture!
And though the fields look rough with hoary dew,
All will be gay when noontide wakes anew
The buttercups, the little children's dower
20   —Far brighter than this gaudy melon-flower!

Home-Thoughts, from the Sea

NOBLY, nobly Cape Saint Vincent to the Northwest died away;
Sunset ran, one glorious blood-red, reeking into Cadiz Bay;
Bluish 'mid the burning water, full in face Trafalgar lay;
In the dimmest Northeast distance dawned Gibraltar grand
    and gray;
"Here and here did England help me: how can I help
    England?"—say,
Whoso turns as I, this evening, turn to God to praise and pray,
While Jove's planet rises yonder, silent over Africa.

1 **Cape Saint Vincent** the southwestern point of Portugal, where the
Spanish fleet surrendered to Nelson in 1797   3 **Trafalgar** the cape near
Cadiz, Spain, where Nelson defeated the French and Spanish fleets in
1805, and received his death-wound   7 **Jove's planet** Jupiter

The Bishop Orders His Tomb at Saint Praxed's Church

ROME, 15—

VANITY, saith the preacher, vanity! *"what is life!"*
Draw round my bed: is Anselm keeping back? *what is it*
Nephews—sons mine ... ah God, I know not! Well— *all about*
She, men would have to be your mother once, *his no law'ful*
Old Gandolf envied me, so fair she was! *children*
What 's done is done, and she is dead beside,
Dead long ago, and I am Bishop since,
And as she died so must we die ourselves,
And thence ye may perceive the world 's a dream.
Life, how and what is it? As here I lie   10
In this state-chamber, dying by degrees,
Hours and long hours in the dead night, I ask
"Do I live, am I dead?" Peace, peace seems all.
Saint Praxed's ever was the church for peace;
And so, about this tomb of mine. I fought
With tooth and nail to save my niche, ye know:
—Old Gandolf cozened me, despite my care;
Shrewd was that snatch from out the corner South
He graced his carrion with, God curse the same!
Yet my niche is not so cramped but thence   20
One sees the pulpit o' the epistle-side,
And somewhat of the choir, those silent seats,
And up into the aery dome where live
The angels, and a sunbeam 's sure to lurk:
And I shall fill my slab of basalt there,
And 'neath my tabernacle take my rest,
With those nine columns round me, two and two,
The odd one at my feet where Anselm stands:
Peach-blossom marble all, the rare, the ripe
As fresh-poured red wine of a mighty pulse.   30

Title: The Bishop, his tomb, and Gandolf are imaginary. St Praxed's is an
ornamented church in Rome, visited by Browning in 1844, named for
S. Prassede, a Roman virgin of the second century. 1 **Vanity** *See* Ec-
clesiastes 1:2 2 **the epistle-side** the right side as one faces the altar
25 **basalt** a hard black stone 26 **tabernacle** canopy

—Old Gandolf with his paltry onion-stone,
Put me where I may look at him! True peach,
Rosy and flawless: how I earned the prize!
Draw close: that conflagration of my church
—What then? So much was saved if aught were missed!
My sons, ye would not be my death? Go dig
The white-grape vineyard where the oil press stood,
Drop water gently till the surface sink,
And if you find ... Ah God, I know not, I! ...
40   Bedded in store of rotten fig leaves soft,
And corded up in a tight olive-frail,
Some lump, ah God, of *lapis lazuli,*
Big as a Jew's head cut off at the nape,
Blue as a vein o'er the Madonna's breast ...
Sons, all have I bequeathed you, villas, all,
That brave Frascati villa with its bath,
So, let the blue lump poise between my knees,
Like God the Father's globe on both his hands
Ye worship in the Jesu Church so gay,
50   For Gandolf shall not choose but see and burst!
Swift as a weaver's shuttle fleet our years:
Man goeth to the grave, and where is he?
Did I say basalt for my slab, sons? Black—
'T was ever antique-black I meant! How else
Shall ye contrast my frieze to come beneath?
The bas-relief in bronze ye promised me,
Those Pans and Nymphs ye wot of, and perchance
Some tripod, thyrsus, with a vase or so,
The Saviour at his sermon on the mount,
60   Saint Praxed in a glory, and one Pan
Ready to twitch the Nymph's last garment off,
And Moses with the tables ... but I know
Ye mark me not! What do they whisper thee,
Child of my bowels, Anselm? Ah, ye hope
To revel down my villas while I gasp
Bricked o'er with beggar's moldy travertine

[handwritten marginal note beside lines 59-60: "only religious ..."]

31 **onion-stone** a cheap greenish marble that peels in layers 41 **frail** basket 42 **lapis lazuli** a semiprecious blue stone 46 **Frascati** a wealthy suburb, twelve miles southeast of Rome 49 **Jesu Church** Il Jesu, the Jesuit church in Rome 51 **Swift as a weaver's shuttle** Job VII:6 58 **tripod** a three-footed stool, connected with the rites of the Delphic Oracle **thyrsus** a staff associated with Bacchus 62 **Moses with the tables** the stone tablets containing the ten commandments. Exodus XXIV. 66 **travertine** a cheap flaky stone

Which Gandolf from his tomb-top chuckles at!
Nay, boys, ye love me—all of jasper, then!
'T is jasper ye stand pledged to, lest I grieve.
My bath must needs be left behind, alas!   70
One block, pure green as a pistachio nut,
There 's plenty jasper somewhere in the world—
And have I not Saint Praxed's ear to pray
Horses for ye, and brown Greek manuscripts,
And mistresses with great smooth marbly limbs?
—That 's if ye carve my epitaph aright,
Choice Latin, picked phrase, Tully's every word,
No gaudy ware like Gandolf's second line—
Tully, my masters? Ulpian serves his need!
And then how I shall lie through centuries,   80
And hear the blessed mutter of the mass,
And see God made and eaten all day long,
And feel the steady candle-flame, and taste
Good strong thick stupefying incense smoke!
For as I lie here, hours of the dead night,
Dying in state and by such slow degrees,
I fold my arms as if they clasped a crook,
And stretch my feet forth straight as stone can point,
And let the bedclothes, for a mortcloth, drop
Into great laps and folds of sculptor's-work: 90
And as yon tapers dwindle, and strange thoughts
Grow, with a certain humming in my ears,
About the life before I lived this life,
And this life too, popes, cardinals and priests,
Saint Praxed at his sermon on the mount,
Your tall pale mother with her talking eyes,
And new-found agate urns as fresh as day,
And marble's language, Latin pure, discreet,
—Aha, ELUCESCEBAT quoth our friend?
No Tully, said I, Ulpian at the best!   100
Evil and brief hath been my pilgrimage.
All *lapis,* all, sons! Else I give the Pope
My villas! Will ye ever eat my heart?

77 Tully Marcus Tullius Cicero   **79 Ulpian** Domitius Ulpianus (170-228
A.D.), a learned jurist whose Latin is not classical   **82 God made and eaten**
in the sacrament of the mass   **87 crook** a crozier, a symbol of the bishop's
rank   **89 mortcloth** funeral pall   **95 Saint Praxed at his sermon** S. Prassede was a virgin; the Bishop's mind wanders   **99 elucescebat** decadent
Latin for the classical form *elucebat.* meaning "he was illustrious"

Ever your eyes were as a lizard's quick,
They glitter like your mother's for my soul,
Or you would heighten my impoverished frieze,
Piece out its starved design, and fill my vase
With grapes, and add a vizor and a Term,
And to the tripod ye would tie a lynx
110   That in his struggle throws the thyrsus down,
To comfort me on my entablature
Whereon I am to lie till I must ask
"Do I live, am I dead?" There, leave me, there!
For ye have stabbed me with ingratitude
To death—ye wish it—God, ye wish it! Stone—
Gritstone, a-crumble! Clammy squares which sweat
As if the corpse they keep were oozing through—
And no more *lapis* to delight the world!
Well, go! I bless ye. Fewer tapers there,
120   But in a row: and, going, turn your backs
—Ay, like departing altar-ministrants,
And leave me in my church, the church for peace,
That I may watch at leisure if he leers—
Old Gandolf, at me, from his onion-stone,
As still he envied me, so fair she was!

Meeting at Night

I

THE grey sea and the long black land;
And the yellow half-moon large and low;
And the startled little waves that leap
In fiery ringlets from their sleep,
As I gain the cove with pushing prow,
And quench its speed i' the slushy sand.

II

Then a mile of warm sea-scented beach;
Three fields to cross till a farm appears;
A tap at the pane, the quick sharp scratch

108 vizor a mask. Term a bust on a pedestal   116 gritstone a cheap
coarse sandstone

And blue spurt of a lighted match,   10
And a voice less loud, thro' its joys and fears,
Than the two hearts beating each to each!

Parting at Morning

ROUND the cape of a sudden came the sea,
And the sun looked over the mountain's rim:
And straight was a path of gold for him,
And the need of a world of men for me.

Love Among the Ruins

I

WHERE the quiet-colored end of evening smiles
            Miles and miles
On the solitary pastures where our sheep
            Half-asleep
Tinkle homeward thro' the twilight, stray or stop
            As they crop—
Was the site once of a city great and gay,
            (So they say)
Of our country's very capital, its prince
            Ages since   10
Held his court in, gathered councils, wielding far
            Peace or war.

II

Now,—the country does not even boast a tree
            As you see,
To distinguish slopes of verdure, certain rills
            From the hills
Intersect and give a name to, (else they run
            Into one)
Where the domed and daring palace shot its spires
            Up like fires   20

3 him the sun

O'er the hundred-gated circuit of a wall
           Bounding all,
Made of marble, men might march on nor be pressed,
           Twelve abreast.

III

And such plenty and perfection, see, of grass
           Never was!
Such a carpet as, this summertime, o'erspreads
           And embeds
Every vestige of the city, guessed alone,
30   Stock or stone—
Where a multitude of men breathed joy and woe
           Long ago;
Lust of glory pricked their hearts up, dread of shame
           Struck them tame;
And that glory and that shame alike, the gold
           Bought and sold.

IV

Now,—the single little turret that remains
           On the plains,
By the caper overrooted, by the gourd
40   Overscored,
While the patching houseleek's head of blossom winks
           Through the chinks—
Marks the basement whence a tower in ancient time
           Sprang sublime,
And a burning ring, all round, the chariots traced
           As they raced,
And the monarch and his minions and his dames
           Viewed the games.

V

And I know, while thus the quiet-colored eve
50   Smiles to leave
To their folding, all our many-tinkling fleece
           In such peace,
And the slopes and rills in undistinguished grey
           Melt away—

39 caper a low prickly bush 41 **houseleek** a small spreading plant 47 **minions** creatures, favorites

That a girl with eager eyes and yellow hair
        Waits me there
In the turret whence the charioteers caught soul
        For the goal,
When the king looked, where she looks now, breathless, dumb
        Till I come.   60

VI

But he looked upon the city, every side,
        Far and wide,
All the mountains topped with temples, all the glades'
        Colonnades,
All the causeys, bridges, aqueducts,—and then,
        All the men!
When I do come, she will speak not, she will stand,
        Either hand
On my shoulder, give her eyes the first embrace
        Of my face,   70
Ere we rush, ere we extinguish sight and speech
        Each on each.

VII

In one year they sent a million fighters forth
        South and North,
And they built their gods a brazen pillar high
        As the sky,
Yet reserved a thousand chariots in full force—
        Gold, of course.
Oh heart! oh blood that freezes, blood that burns!
        Earth's returns   80
For whole centuries of folly, noise and sin!
        Shut them in,
With their triumphs and their glories and the rest!
        Love is best.

65 **causeys** causeways, raised paths

Up at a Villa—Down in the City

AS DISTINGUISHED BY AN ITALIAN PERSON OF QUALITY

I

HAD I but plenty of money, money enough and to spare,
The house for me, no doubt, were a house in the city square;
Ah, such a life, such a life, as one leads at the window there!

II

Something to see, by Bacchus, something to hear, at least!
There, the whole day long, one's life is a perfect feast;
While up at a villa one lives, I maintain it, no more than a
   beast.

III

Well now, look at our villa! stuck like the horn of a bull
Just on a mountain-edge as bare as the creature's skull,
Save a mere shag of a bush with hardly a leaf to pull!
—I scratch my own, sometimes, to see if the hair 's turned
   wool.

IV

But the city, oh the city—the square with the houses! Why?
They are stone-faced, white as a curd, there 's something to
   take the eye!
Houses in four straight lines, not a single front awry;
You watch who crosses and gossips, who saunters, who hurries
   by;
Green blinds, as a matter of course, to draw when the sun gets
   high;
And the shops with fanciful signs which are painted properly.

V

What of a villa? Though winter be over in March by rights,
'T is May perhaps ere the snow shall have withered well off
   the heights:
You 've the brown ploughed land before, where the oxen
   steam and wheeze,
And the hills oversmoked behind by the faint grey olive trees.

VI

Is it better in May, I ask you? You 've summer all at once;
In a day he leaps complete with a few strong April suns.
'Mid the sharp short emerald wheat, scarce risen three fingers
    well,
The wild tulip, at end of its tube, blows out its great red bell
Like a thin clear bubble of blood, for the children to pick and
    sell.

VII

Is it ever hot in the square? There 's a fountain to spout and
    splash!
In the shade it sings and springs; in the shine such foam-bows
    flash
On the horses with curling fishtails, that prance and paddle
    and pash
Round the lady atop in her conch—fifty gazers do not abash,
Though all that she wears is some weeds round her waist in a
    sort of sash.   30

VIII

All the year long at the villa, nothing to see though you linger,
Except yon cypress that points like death's lean lifted fore-
    finger.
Some think fireflies pretty, when they mix i' the corn and
    mingle,
Or thrid the stinking hemp till the stalks of it seem a-tingle.
Late August or early September, the stunning cicala is shrill,
And the bees keep their tiresome whine round the resinous
    firs on the hill.
Enough of the seasons,—I spare you the months of the fever
    and chill.

IX

Ere you open your eyes in the city, the blessed church bells
    begin:
No sooner the bells leave off than the diligence rattles in:
You get the pick of the news, and it costs you never a pin.   40
By-and-by there 's the travelling doctor gives pills, lets blood,
    draws teeth;
Or the Pulcinello-trumpet breaks up the market beneath.

29 **conch** shell   42 **Pulcinello-trumpet** the trumpet blown to announce the
coming of the puppet-show. Pulcinello is the Italian ancestor of Punch,
of Punch and Judy.

At the post office such a scene-picture—the new play, piping
 hot!

And a notice how, only this morning, three liberal thieves
 were shot.

Above it, behold the Archbishop's most fatherly of rebukes,

And beneath, with his crown and his lion, some little new law
 of the Duke's!

Or a sonnet with flowery marge, to the Reverend Don So-
 and-so

Who is Dante, Boccaccio, Petrarca, Saint Jerome and Cicero,

"And moreover," (the sonnet goes rhyming,) "the skirts of
 Saint Paul has reached,

50 "Having preached us those six Lent-lectures more unctuous
 than ever he preached."

Noon strikes,—here sweeps the procession! our Lady borne
 smiling and smart

With a pink gauze gown all spangles, and seven swords stuck
 in her heart!

Bang-whang-whang goes the drum, *tootle-te-tootle* the fife;

No keeping one's haunches still: it's the greatest pleasure in
 life.

                    x

But bless you, it's dear—it's dear! fowls, wine, at double the
 rate.

They have clapped a new tax upon salt, and what oil pays
 passing the gate

It's a horror to think of. And so, the villa for me, not the city!

Beggars can scarcely be choosers: but still—ah, the pity, the
 pity!

Look, two and two go the priests, then the monks with cowls
 and sandals,

60 And the penitents dressed in white shirts, a-holding the yellow
 candles;

One, he carries a flag up straight, and another a cross with
 handles,

And the Duke's guard brings up the rear, for the better pre-
 vention of scandals:

Bang-whang-whang goes the drum, *tootle-te-tootle* the fife.

Oh, a day in the city square, there is no such pleasure in life!

---

43 **scene-picture** a poster giving previews of the coming play 44 **liberal
thieves** men of the revolutionary party against Austria, who combined
their resistance with thievery 51 **our Lady** the Virgin, here Our Lady of
Sorrows. The seven swords represent the seven great sorrows of her life.

Fra Lippo Lippi

I AM poor brother Lippo, by your leave!
You need not clap your torches to my face.
Zooks, what 's to blame? you think you see a monk!
What, 't is past midnight, and you go the rounds,
And here you catch me at an alley's end
Where sportive ladies leave their doors ajar?
The Carmine 's my cloister: hunt it up
Do,—harry out, if you must show your zeal,
Whatever rat, there, haps on his wrong hole,
And nip each softling of a wee white mouse,   10
Weke, weke, that 's crept to keep him company!
Aha, you know your betters! Then, you 'll take
Your hand away that 's fiddling on my throat,
And please to know me likewise. Who am I?
Why, one, sir, who is lodging with a friend
Three streets off—he 's a certain . . . how d' ye call?
Master—a . . . Cosimo of the Medici,
I' the house that caps the corner. Boh! you were best!
Remember and tell me, the day you 're hanged,
How you affected such a gullet's-gripe!   20
But you, sir, it concerns you that your knaves
Pick up a manner nor discredit you:
Zooks, are we pilchards, that they sweep the streets
And count fair prize what comes into their net?
He 's Judas to a title, that man is!
Just such a face! Why, sir, you make amends.
Lord, I 'm not angry! Bid your hangdogs go
Drink out this quarter-florin to the health
Of the munificent House that harbors me
(And many more beside, lads! more beside!)   30
And all 's come square again. I 'd like his face—
His, elbowing on his comrade in the door
With the pike and lantern,—for the slave that holds

Title: See Vasari's *Lives of the Painters,* which Browning mainly followed
in his account of Lippi's life (1406-69)   3 **Zooks** a mild oath   6 **sportive
ladies** prostitutes   7 **Carmine** the monastery of the Carmelites   17 **Cosimo
of the Medici** Cosimo (1389-1464) was the great banker, statesman, and
patron of the arts   23 **pilchards** small fish

John Baptist's head a-dangle by the hair
With one hand ("Look you, now," as who would say)
And his weapon in the other, yet unwiped!
It 's not your chance to have a bit of chalk,
A wood-coal or the like? or you should see!
Yes, I 'm the painter, since you style me so.
40 What, brother Lippo's doings, up and down,
You know them and they take you? like enough!
I saw the proper twinkle in your eye—
'Tell you, I liked your looks at very first.
Let 's sit and set things straight now, hip to haunch.
Here 's spring come, and the nights one makes up bands
To roam the town and sing out carnival,
And I 've been three weeks shut within my mew,
A-painting for the great man, saints and saints
And saints again. I could not paint all night—
50 Ouf! I leaned out of window for fresh air.
There came a hurry of feet and little feet,
A sweep of lute strings, laughs, and whiffs of song,—
Flower o' the broom,
Take away love, and our earth is a tomb!
Flower o' the quince,
I let Lisa go, and what good in life since?
Flower o' the thyme—and so on. Round they went.
Scarce had they turned the corner when a titter
Like the skipping of rabbits by moonlight,—three slim shapes,
60 And a face that looked up . . . zooks, sir, flesh and blood,
That 's all I 'm made of! Into shreds it went,
Curtain and counterpane and coverlet,
All the bed-furniture—a dozen knots,
There was a ladder! Down I let myself,
Hands and feet, scrambling somehow, and so dropped,
And after them. I came up with the fun
Hard by Saint Laurence, hail fellow, well met,—
Flower o' the rose,
If I 've been merry, what matter who knows?
70 And so as I was stealing back again
To get to bed and have a bit of sleep
Ere I rise up tomorrow and go work

34 **John Baptist's head** according to Vasari, a favorite theme of Lippi's
67 **Saint Laurence** the church of San Lorenzo in Florence

On Jerome knocking at his poor old breast
With his great round stone to subdue the flesh,
You snap me of the sudden. Ah, I see!
Though your eye twinkles still, you shake your head—
Mine 's shaved—a monk, you say—the sting 's in that!
If Master Cosimo announced himself,
Mum 's the word naturally; but a monk!
Come, what am I a beast for? tell us, now!   80
I was a baby when my mother died
And father died and left me in the street.
I starved there, God knows how, a year or two
On fig skins, melon parings, rinds and shucks,
Refuse and rubbish. One fine frosty day,
My stomach being empty as your hat,
The wind doubled me up and down I went.
Old Aunt Lapaccia trussed me with one hand,
(Its fellow was a stinger as I knew)
And so along the wall, over the bridge,   90
By the straight cut to the convent. Six words there,
While I stood munching my first bread that month:
"So, boy, you 're minded," quoth the good fat father
Wiping his own mouth, 't was refection-time,—
"To quit this very miserable world?
"Will you renounce" ... "the mouthful of bread?" thought I;
By no means! Brief, they made a monk of me;
I did renounce the world, its pride and greed,
Palace, farm, villa, shop and banking house,
Trash, such as these poor devils of Medici   100
Have given their hearts to—all at eight years old.
Well, sir, I found in time, you may be sure,
'T was not for nothing—the good bellyful,
The warm serge and the rope that goes all round,
And day-long blessed idleness beside!
"Let 's see what the urchin 's fit for"—that came next.
Not overmuch their way, I must confess.
Such a to-do! They tried me with their books:
Lord, they 'd have taught me Latin in pure waste!
Flower o' the clove,   110
All the Latin I construe is, "amo" I love!
But, mind you, when a boy starves in the streets

73 **Jerome** Saint Jerome (340-420), a learned church father who lived in
the desert as penance for his sins   88 **Aunt Lapaccia** Lippi's father's sister,
who took care of the painter in his youth

Eight years together, as my fortune was,
Watching folk's faces to know who will fling
The bit of half-stripped grape bunch he desires,
And who will curse or kick him for his pains,—
Which gentleman processional and fine,
Holding a candle to the Sacrament,
Will wink and let him lift a plate and catch
120 The droppings of the wax to sell again,
Or holla for the Eight and have him whipped,—
How say I?—nay, which dog bites, which lets drop
His bone from the heap of offal in the street,—
Why, soul and sense of him grow sharp alike,
He learns the look of things, and nonetheless
For admonition from the hunger-pinch.
I had a store of such remarks, be sure,
Which, after I found leisure, turned to use.
I drew men's faces on my copybooks,
130 Scrawled them within the antiphonary's marge,
Joined legs and arms to the long music notes,
Found eyes and nose and chin for A's and B's,
And made a string of pictures of the world
Betwixt the ins and outs of verb and noun,
On the wall, the bench, the door. The monks looked black.
"Nay," quoth the Prior, "turn him out, d' ye say?
"In no wise. Lose a crow and catch a lark.
"What if at last we get our man of parts,
"We Carmelites, like those Camaldolese
140 "And Preaching Friars, to do our church up fine
"And put the front on it that ought to be!"
And hereupon he bade me daub away.
Thank you! my head being crammed, the walls a blank,
Never was such prompt disemburdening.
First, every sort of monk, the black and white,
I drew them, fat and lean: then, folk at church,
From good old gossips waiting to confess
Their cribs of barrel-droppings, candle ends,—
To the breathless fellow at the altar foot,
150 Fresh from his murder, safe and sitting there

117 **gentlemen processional and fine** gentlemen clothed in ecclesiastical robes, walking in procession   121 **the Eight** the magistrates of Florence   130 **antiphonary** book containing the responses used by the choirboys   139 **Camaldolese** a religious order established at the convent of the Camaldi, near Florence; less important than the Carmelites or the Dominicans, the Preaching Friars   148 **cribs** small thefts

Are peeping o'er my shoulder as I work,
The heads shake still—"It 's art's decline, my son!
"You 're not of the true painters, great and old;
"Brother Angelico 's the man, you 'll find;
"Brother Lorenzo stands his single peer:
"Fag on at flesh, you 'll never make the third!"
Flower o' the pine,
You keep your mistr . . . manners, and I 'll stick to mine!
I 'm not the third, then: bless us, they must know!   240
Don't you think they 're the likeliest to know,
They with their Latin? So, I swallow my rage,
Clench my teeth, suck my lips in tight, and paint
To please them—sometimes do and sometimes don't;
For, doing most, there 's pretty sure to come
A turn, some warm eve finds me at my saints—
A laugh, a cry, the business of the world—
(*Flower o' the peach,*
Death for us all, and his own life for each!)
And my whole soul revolves, the cup runs over,   250
The world and life 's too big to pass for a dream,
And I do these wild things in sheer despite,
And play the fooleries you catch me at,
In pure rage! The old mill-horse, out at grass
After hard years, throws up his stiff heels so,
Although the miller does not preach to him
The only good of grass is to make chaff.
What would men have? Do they like grass or no—
May they or mayn't they? all I want 's the thing
Settled for ever one way. As it is,   260
You tell too many lies and hurt yourself:
You don't like what you only like too much,
You do like what, if given you at your word,
You find abundantly detestable.
For me, I think I speak as I was taught;
I always see the garden and God there
A-making man's wife: and, my lesson learned,
The value and significance of flesh,
I can't unlearn ten minutes afterwards.

You understand me: I 'm a beast, I know.   270
But see, now—why, I see as certainly
As that the morning star 's about to shine,
What will hap some day. We 've a youngster here

Comes to our convent, studies what I do,
Slouches and stares and lets no atom drop:
His name is Guidi—he 'll not mind the monks—
They call him Hulking Tom, he lets them talk—
He picks my practice up—he 'll paint apace,
I hope so—though I never live so long,
280 I know what 's sure to follow. You be judge!
You speak no Latin more than I, belike;
However, you 're my man, you 've seen the world
—The beauty and the wonder and the power,
The shapes of things, their colors, lights and shades,
Changes, surprises,—and God made it all!
—For what? Do you feel thankful, ay or no,
For this fair town's face, yonder river's line,
The mountain round it and the sky above,
Much more the figures of man, woman, child,
290 These are the frame to? What 's it all about?
To be passed over, despised? or dwelt upon,
Wondered at? oh, this last of course!—you say.
But why not do as well as say,—paint these
Just as they are, careless what comes of it?
God's works—paint any one, and count it crime
To let a truth slip. Don't object, "His works
"Are here already; nature is complete:
"Suppose you reproduce her—(which you can't)
"There 's no advantage! you must beat her, then."
300 For, don't you mark? we 're made so that we love
First when we see them painted, things we have passed
Perhaps a hundred times nor cared to see;
And so they are better, painted—better to us,
Which is the same thing. Art was given for that;
God uses us to help each other so,
Lending our minds out. Have you noticed, now,
Your cullion's hanging face? A bit of chalk,
And trust me but you should, though! How much more,
If I drew higher things with the same truth!
310 That were to take the Prior's pulpit-place,
Interpret God to all of you! Oh, oh,
It makes me mad to see what men shall do
And we in our graves! This world 's no blot for us,
Nor blank; it means intensely, and means good:

276 **Guidi** Tommaso Guidi or Masaccio (1401-28). Browning was mistaken in thinking "Hulking Tom" a pupil of Lippi's.   307 **cullion** rascal

To find its meaning is my meat and drink.
"Ay, but you don't so instigate to prayer!"
Strikes in the Prior: "when your meaning 's plain
"It does not say to folk—remember matins,
"Or, mind you fast next Friday!" Why, for this
What need of art at all? A skull and bones,   320
Two bits of stick nailed crosswise, or, what 's best,
A bell to chime the hour with, does as well.
I painted a Saint Laurence six months since
At Prato, splashed the fresco in fine style:
"How looks my painting, now the scaffold 's down?"
I ask a brother: "Hugely," he returns—
"Already not one phiz of your three slaves
"Who turn the Deacon off his toasted side,
"But 's scratched and prodded to our heart's content,
"The pious people have so eased their own   330
"With coming to say prayers there in a rage:
"We get on fast to see the bricks beneath.
"Expect another job this time next year,
"For pity and religion grow i' the crowd—
"Your painting serves its purpose!" Hang the fools!
—That is—you 'll not mistake an idle word
Spoke in a huff by a poor monk, God wot,
Tasting the air this spicy night which turns
The unaccustomed head like Chianti wine!
Oh, the church knows! don't misreport me, now!   340
It 's natural a poor monk out of bounds
Should have his apt word to excuse himself:
And hearken how I plot to make amends.
I have bethought me: I shall paint a piece
... There 's for you! Give me six months, then go, see
Something in Sant' Ambrogio's! Bless the nuns!
They want a cast o' my office. I shall paint
God in the midst, Madonna and her babe,
Ringed by a bowery flowery angel-brood,
Lilies and vestments and white faces, sweet   350
As puff on puff of grated orrisroot
When ladies crowd to Church at midsummer.

---

323 **Saint Laurence** Laurence was roasted on a gridiron in 258   324 **Prato**
some of Lippi's greatest work is in the church at Prato, a town near
Florence   327 **phiz** face   339 **Chianti** a famous wine from the district
south of Florence   346 **Sant' Ambrogio's** the church in Florence for
which Lippi was to paint the Coronation of the Virgin

And then i' the front, of course a saint or two—
Saint John, because he saves the Florentines,
Saint Ambrose, who puts down in black and white
The convent's friends and gives them a long day,
And Job, I must have him there past mistake,
The man of Uz (and Us without the z,
Painters who need his patience). Well, all these
360 Secured at their devotion, up shall come
Out of a corner when you least expect,
As one by a dark stair into a great light,
Music and talking, who but Lippo! I!—
Mazed, motionless and moonstruck—I 'm the man!
Back I shrink—what is this I see and hear?
I, caught up with my monk's-things by mistake,
My old serge gown and rope that goes all round,
I, in this presence, this pure company!
Where 's a hole, where 's a corner for escape?
370 Then steps a sweet angelic slip of a thing
Forward, puts out a soft palm—"Not so fast!"
—Addresses the celestial presence, "nay—
"He made you and devised you, after all,
"Though he 's none of you! Could Saint John there draw—
"His camel-hair make up a painting brush?
"We come to brother Lippo for all that,
"*Iste perfecit opus!*" So, all smile—
I shuffle sideways with my blushing face
Under the cover of a hundred wings
380 Thrown like a spread of kirtles when you 're gay
And play hot cockles, all the doors being shut,
Till, wholly unexpected, in there pops
The hothead husband! Thus I scuttle off
To some safe bench behind, not letting go
The palm of her, the little lily thing
That spoke the good word for me in the nick,
Like the Prior's niece . . . Saint Lucy, I would say.
And so all 's saved for me, and for the church
A pretty picture gained. Go, six months hence!
390 Your hand, sir, and goodbye: no lights, no lights!
The street 's hushed, and I know my own way back,
Don't fear me! there 's the grey beginning. Zooks!

363 **Lippo** Browning was mistaken in his identification of Lippi in the
picture   377 **"Iste perfecit opus"** This man made the work   381 **hot
cockles** a game like blindman's buff

A Toccata of Galuppi's

I

OH Galuppi, Baldassaro, this is very sad to find!
I can hardly misconceive you; it would prove me deaf and
blind;
But although I take your meaning, 't is with such a heavy
mind!

II

Here you come with your old music, and here 's all the good
it brings.
What, they lived once thus at Venice where the merchants
were the kings,
Where Saint Mark's is, where the Doges used to wed the sea
with rings?

III

Ay, because the sea 's the street there; and 't is arched by . . .
what you call
. . . Shylock's bridge with houses on it, where they kept the
carnival:
I was never out of England—it 's as if I saw it all.

IV

Did young people take their pleasure when the sea was warm
in May?   10
Balls and masks begun at midnight, burning ever to midday,
When they made up fresh adventures for the morrow, do you
say?

V

Was a lady such a lady, cheeks so round and lips so red,—
On her neck the small face buoyant, like a bellflower on its bed,
O'er the breast's superb abundance where a man might base
his head?

1 **Galuppi** Baldassaro Galuppi (1706-85) was a Venetian organist and
composer of light opera. A toccata is a touch-piece, light in tone and free
in movement, a preliminary flourish or overture illustrating technique.
6 **Saint Mark's** the great cathedral at Venice **Doges** the chief magistrate
of the city was the Doge **wed the sea** an annual ceremony, in which the
wedding of Venice to the Adriatic was symbolized by the Doge casting a
ring into the sea 8 **Shylock's bridge** the Rialto, the great bridge over the
Grand Canal

VI

Well, and it was graceful of them—they 'd break talk off and
afford
—She, to bite her mask's black velvet—he, to finger on his
sword,
While you sat and played Toccatas, stately at the clavichord?

VII

What? Those lesser thirds so plaintive, sixths diminished, sigh
on sigh,
Told them something? Those suspensions, those solutions—
20   "Must we die?"
Those commiserating sevenths—"Life might last! we can but
try!"

VIII

"Were you happy?"—"Yes."—"And are you still as happy?"
—"Yes. And you?"
—"Then, more kisses!"—"Did *I* stop them, when a million
seemed so few?"
Hark, the dominant's persistence till it must be answered to!

IX

So, an octave struck the answer. Oh, they praised you, I dare
say!
"Brave Galuppi! that was music! good alike at grave and gay!
"I can always leave off talking when I hear a master play!"

X

Then they left you for their pleasure: till in due time, one by
one,
Some with lives that came to nothing, some with deeds as
well undone,
Death stepped tacitly and took them where they never see the
30   sun.

XI

But when I sit down to reason, think to take my stand nor
swerve,
While I triumph o'er a secret wrung from nature's close
reserve,
In you come with your cold music till I creep thro' every nerve.

18 **clavichord** an instrument of keys and strings, ancestor of the modern
piano

XII

Yes, you, like a ghostly cricket, creaking where a house was
  burned:
"Dust and ashes, dead and done with, Venice spent what
  Venice earned.
"The soul, doubtless, is immortal—where a soul can be dis-
  cerned.

XIII

"Yours for instance: you know physics, something of geology,
"Mathematics are your pastime; souls shall rise in their degree;
"Butterflies may dread extinction,—you' ll not die, it cannot
  be!

XIV

"As for Venice and her people, merely born to bloom and
  drop,
"Here on earth they bore their fruitage, mirth and folly were
  the crop:
"What of soul was left, I wonder, when the kissing had to
  stop?

XV

"Dust and ashes!" So you creak it, and I want the heart to
  scold.
Dear dead women, with such hair, too—what 's become of all
  the gold
Used to hang and brush their bosoms? I feel chilly and grown
  old.

40

An Epistle

CONTAINING THE STRANGE MEDICAL EXPERIENCE
OF KARSHISH, THE ARAB PHYSICIAN

KARSHISH, the picker-up of learning's crumbs,
The not-incurious in God's handiwork
(This man's-flesh he hath admirably made,
Blown like a bubble, kneaded like a paste,
To coop up and keep down on earth a space
That puff of vapor from his mouth, man's soul)

Title: The characters of Karshish and Abib are imaginary. The action of
the poem is supposed to have taken place in 66 A.D. when the Emperor
Vespasian invaded Palestine.

—To Abib, all-sagacious in our art,
Breeder in me of what poor skill I boast,
Like me inquisitive how pricks and cracks
Befall the flesh through too much stress and strain,
Whereby the wily vapor fain would slip
Back and rejoin its source before the term,—
And aptest in contrivance (under God)
To baffle it by deftly stopping such:—
The vagrant Scholar to his Sage at home
Sends greeting (health and knowledge, fame with peace)
Three samples of true snakestone—rarer still,
One of the other sort, the melon-shaped,
(But fitter, pounded fine, for charms than drugs)
And writeth now the twenty-second time.

My journeyings were brought to Jericho:
Thus I resume. Who studious in our art
Shall count a little labor unrepaid?
I have shed sweat enough, left flesh and bone
On many a flinty furlong of this land.
Also, the countryside is all on fire
With rumors of a marching hitherward:
Some say Vespasian cometh, some, his son.
A black lynx snarled and pricked a tufted ear;
Lust of my blood inflamed his yellow balls:
I cried and threw my staff and he was gone.
Twice have the robbers stripped and beaten me,
And once a town declared me for a spy;
But at the end, I reach Jerusalem,
Since this poor covert where I pass the night,
This Bethany, lies scarce the distance thence
A man with plague-sores at the third degree
Runs till he drops down dead. Thou laughest here!
'Sooth, it elates me, thus reposed and safe,
To void the stuffing of my travel-scrip
And share with thee whatever Jewry yields.
A viscid choler is observable
In tertians, I was nearly bold to say;
And falling-sickness hath a happier cure

---

17 **snakestone** a stone used to cure snake bites   28 **his son** Vespasian's son,
Titus, who destroyed Jerusalem in 70 A.D.   42 **viscid choler** a sticky,
heated condition   43 **tertians** fevers recurring every third day   44 **falling-
sickness** epilepsy

Than our school wots of: there 's a spider here
Weaves no web, watches on the ledge of tombs,
Sprinkled with mottles on an ash-grey back;
Take five and drop them ... but who knows his mind,
The Syrian runagate I trust this to?
His service payeth me a sublimate   50
Blown up his nose to help the ailing eye.
Best wait: I reach Jerusalem at morn,
There set in order my experiences,
Gather what most deserves, and give thee all—
Or I might add, Judaea's gum tragacanth
Scales off in purer flakes, shines clearer-grained,
Cracks 'twixt the pestle and the porphyry,
In fine exceeds our produce. Scalp disease
Confounds me, crossing so with leprosy—
Thou hadst admired one sort I gained at Zoar—   60
But zeal outruns discretion. Here I end.

Yet stay: my Syrian blinketh gratefully,
Protesteth his devotion is my price—
Suppose I write what harms not, though he steal?
I half resolve to tell thee, yet I blush,
What set me off a-writing first of all.
An itch I had, a sting to write, a tang!
For, be it this town's barrenness—or else
The Man had something in the look of him—
His case has struck me far more than 't is worth.   70
So, pardon if—(lest presently I lose
In the great press of novelty at hand
The care and pains this somehow stole from me)
I bid thee take the thing while fresh in mind,
Almost in sight—for, wilt thou have the truth?
The very man is gone from me but now,
Whose ailment is the subject of discourse.
Thus then, and let thy better wit help all!

'T is but a case of mania—subinduced
By epilepsy, at the turning point   80
Of trance prolonged unduly some three days:
When, by the exhibition of some drug

55 **gum tragacanth** medicinal gum from a shrub 60 **Zoar** a city near the
Dead Sea 69 **The Man** Lazarus. *See* John XI:1-44 82 **exhibition** application

Or spell, exorcization, stroke of art
Unknown to me and which 't were well to know,
The evil thing outbreaking all at once
Left the man whole and sound of body indeed,—
But, flinging (so to speak) life's gates too wide,
Making a clear house of it too suddenly,
The first conceit that entered might inscribe
90 Whatever it was minded on the wall
So plainly at that vantage, as it were,
(First come, first served) that nothing subsequent
Attaineth to erase those fancy-scrawls
The just-returned and new-established soul
Hath gotten now so thoroughly by heart
That henceforth she will read or these or none.
And first—the man's own firm conviction rests
That he was dead (in fact they buried him)
—That he was dead and then restored to life
100 By a Nazarene physician of his tribe:
—'Sayeth, the same bade "Rise," and he did rise.
"Such cases are diurnal," thou wilt cry.
Not so this figment!—not, that such a fume,
Instead of giving way to time and health,
Should eat itself into the life of life,
As saffron tingeth flesh, blood, bones and all!
For see, how he takes up the afterlife.
The man—it is one Lazarus a Jew,
Sanguine, proportioned, fifty years of age,
110 The body's habit wholly laudable,
As much, indeed, beyond the common health
As he were made and put aside to show.
Think, could we penetrate by any drug
And bathe the wearied soul and worried flesh,
And bring it clear and fair, by three days' sleep!
Whence has the man the balm that brightens all?
This grown man eyes the world now like a child.
Some elders of his tribe, I should premise,
Led in their friend, obedient as a sheep,
120 To bear my inquisition. While they spoke,
Now sharply, now with sorrow,—told the case,—
He listened not except I spoke to him,

89 conceit notion 93 fancy-scrawls what fantasy has loosely written
100 Nazarene physician Jesus 109 fifty Lazarus would actually have
been about sixty-five at this time

But folded his two hands and let them talk,
Watching the flies that buzzed: and yet no fool.
And that 's a sample how his years must go.
Look, if a beggar, in fixed middle life,
Should find a treasure,—can he use the same
With straitened habits and with tastes starved small,
And take at once to his impoverished brain
The sudden element that changes things,   130
That sets the undreamed-of rapture at his hand
And puts the cheap old joy in the scorned dust?
Is he not such an one as moves to mirth—
Warily parsimonious, when no need,
Wasteful as drunkenness at undue times?
All prudent counsel as to what befits
The golden mean, is lost on such an one:
The man's fantastic will is the man's law.
So here—we call the treasure knowledge, say,
Increased beyond the fleshly faculty—   140
Heaven opened to a soul while yet on earth,
Earth forced on a soul's use while seeing heaven:
The man is witless of the size, the sum,
The value in proportion of all things,
Or whether it be little or be much.
Discourse to him of prodigious armaments
Assembled to besiege his city now,
And of the passing of a mule with gourds—
'T is one! Then take it on the other side,
Speak of some trifling fact,—he will gaze rapt   150
With stupor at its very littleness,
(Far as I see) as if in that indeed
He caught prodigious import, whole results;
And so will turn to us the bystanders
In ever the same stupor (note this point)
That we too see not with his opened eyes.
Wonder and doubt come wrongly into play,
Preposterously, at cross purposes.
Should his child sicken unto death,—why, look
For scarce abatement of his cheerfulness,   160
Or pretermission of the daily craft!
While a word, gesture, glance from that same child
At play or in the school or laid asleep,
Will startle him to an agony of fear,

161 **pretermission** interruption

Exasperation, just as like. Demand
The reason why—"'t is but a word," object—
"A gesture"—he regards thee as our lord,
Who lived there in the pyramid alone,
Looked at us (dost thou mind?) when, being young,
170   We both would unadvisedly recite
Some charm's beginning, from that book of his,
Able to bid the sun throb wide and burst
All into stars, as suns grown old are wont.
Thou and the child have each a veil alike
Thrown o'er your heads, from under which ye both
Stretch your blind hands and trifle with a match
Over a mine of Greek fire, did ye know!
He holds on firmly to some thread of life—
(It is the life to lead perforcedly)
180   Which runs across some vast distracting orb
Of glory on either side that meagre thread,
Which, conscious of, he must not enter yet—
The spiritual life around the earthly life:
The law of that is known to him as this,
His heart and brain move there, his feet stay here.
So is the man perplexed with impulses
Sudden to start off crosswise, not straight on,
Proclaiming what is right and wrong across,
And not along, this black thread through the blaze—
190   "It should be" balked by "here it cannot be."
And oft the man's soul springs into his face
As if he saw again and heard again
His sage that bade him "Rise" and he did rise.
Something, a word, a tick o' the blood within
Admonishes: then back he sinks at once
To ashes, who was very fire before,
In sedulous recurrence to his trade
Whereby he earneth him the daily bread;
And studiously the humbler for that pride,
200   Professedly the faultier that he knows
God's secret, while he holds the thread of life.
Indeed the especial marking of the man
Is prone submission to the heavenly will—
Seeing it, what it is, and why it is.
'Sayeth, he will wait patient to the last

177 **mine of Greek fire** sulphur, nitre and naphtha set ablaze; not used until 673 A.D.

For that same death which must restore his being
To equilibrium, body loosening soul
Divorced even now by premature full growth:
He will live, nay, it pleaseth him to live
So long as God please, and just how God please.   210
He even seeketh not to please God more
(Which meaneth, otherwise) than as God please.
Hence, I perceive not he affects to preach
The doctrine of his sect whate'er it be,
Make proselytes as madmen thirst to do:
How can he give his neighbor the real ground,
His own conviction? Ardent as he is—
Call his great truth a lie, why, still the old
"Be it as God please" reassureth him.
I probed the sore as thy disciple should: 220
"How, beast," said I, "this stolid carelessness
"Sufficeth thee, when Rome is on her march
"To stamp out like a little spark thy town,
"Thy tribe, thy crazy tale and thee at once?"
He merely looked with his large eyes on me.
The man is apathetic, you deduce?
Contrariwise, he loves both old and young,
Able and weak, affects the very brutes
And birds—how say I? flowers of the field—
As a wise workman recognizes tools   230
In a master's workshop, loving what they make.
Thus is the man as harmless as a lamb:
Only impatient, let him do his best,
At ignorance and carelessness and sin—
An indignation which is promptly curbed:
As when in certain travel I have feigned
To be an ignoramus in our art
According to some preconceived design,
And happed to hear the land's practitioners,
Steeped in conceit sublimed by ignorance,   240
Prattle fantastically on disease,
Its cause and cure—and I must hold my peace!

      Thou wilt object—Why have I not ere this
Sought out the sage himself, the Nazarene
Who wrought this cure, inquiring at the source,
Conferring with the frankness that befits?
Alas! it grieveth me, the learned leech

Perished in a tumult many years ago,
Accused,—our learning's fate,—of wizardry,
250   Rebellion, to the setting up a rule
And creed prodigious as described to me.
His death, which happened when the earthquake fell
(Prefiguring, as soon appeared, the loss
To occult learning in our lord the sage
Who lived there in the pyramid alone)
Was wrought by the mad people—that 's their wont!
On vain recourse, as I conjecture it,
To his tried virtue, for miraculous help—
How could he stop the earthquake? That 's their way!
260   The other imputations must be lies:
But take one, though I loathe to give it thee,
In mere respect for any good man's fame.
(And after all, our patient Lazarus
Is stark mad; should we count on what he says?
Perhaps not: though in writing to a leech
'T is well to keep back nothing of a case.)
This man so cured regards the curer, then,
As—God forgive me! who but God himself,
Creator and sustainer of the world,
270   That came and dwelt in flesh on it awhile!
—'Sayeth that such an one was born and lived,
Taught, healed the sick, broke bread at his own house,
Then died, with Lazarus by, for aught I know,
And yet was ... what I said nor choose repeat,
And must have so avouched himself, in fact,
In hearing of this very Lazarus
Who saith—but why all this of what he saith?
Why write of trivial matters, things of price
Calling at every moment for remark?
280   I noticed on the margin of a pool
Blue-flowering borage, the Aleppo sort,
Aboundeth, very nitrous. It is strange!

Thy pardon for this long and tedious case,
Which, now that I review it, needs must seem
Unduly dwelt on, prolixly set forth!
Nor I myself discern in what is writ

252   the earthquake when Jesus hung on the cross. *See* Matthew
XXVII:51   280 **borage** a medicinal plant, supposed to have quickening
powers   **Aleppo** a city in Syria

Good cause for the peculiar interest
And awe indeed this man has touched me with.
Perhaps the journey's end, the weariness
Had wrought upon me first. I met him thus: 290
I crossed a ridge of short sharp broken hills
Like an old lion's cheek teeth. Out there came
A moon made like a face with certain spots
Multiform, manifold and menacing:
Then a wind rose behind me. So we met
In this old sleepy town at unaware,
The man and I. I send thee what is writ.
Regard it as a chance, a matter risked
To this ambiguous Syrian—he may lose,
Or steal, or give it thee with equal good.   300
Jerusalem's repose shall make amends
For time this letter wastes, thy time and mine;
Till when, once more thy pardon and farewell!

The very God! think, Abib; dost thou think?
So, the All-Great, were the All-Loving too—
So, through the thunder comes a human voice
Saying, "O heart I made, a heart beats here!
"Face, my hands fashioned, see it in myself!
"Thou hast no power nor mayst conceive of mine,
"But love I gave thee, with myself to love,   310
"And thou must love me who have died for thee!"
The madman saith He said so: it is strange.

My Star

ALL that I know
    Of a certain star
Is, it can throw
    (Like the angled spar)
Now a dart of red,
    Now a dart of blue;
Till my friends have said
    They would fain see, too,

4 **angled spar** the Iceland prism, which breaks light into its component
colors and reflects the colors at different angles

My star that dartles the red and the blue!
10   Then it stops like a bird; like a flower, hangs furled:
      They must solace themselves with the Saturn above it.
What matter to me if their star is a world?
      Mine has opened its soul to me; therefore I love it.

"Childe Roland to the Dark Tower Came"

(See Edgar's Song in "LEAR")

I

My first thought was, he lied in every word,
      That hoary cripple, with malicious eye
      Askance to watch the working of his lie
On mine, and mouth scarce able to afford
Suppression of the glee, that pursed and scored
      Its edge, at one more victim gained thereby.

II

What else should he be set for, with his staff?
      What, save to waylay with his lies, ensnare
      All travellers who might find him posted there,
10   And ask the road? I guessed what skull-like laugh
Would break, what crutch 'gin write my epitaph
      For pastime in the dusty thoroughfare,

III

If at his counsel I should turn aside
      Into that ominous tract which, all agree,
      Hides the Dark Tower. Yet acquiescingly
I did turn as he pointed: neither pride
Nor hope rekindling at the end descried,
      So much as gladness that some end might be.

IV

For, what with my whole world-wide wandering,
20   What with my search drawn out thro' years, my hope
      Dwindled into a ghost not fit to cope

With that obstreperous joy success would bring,—
I hardly tried now to rebuke the spring
   My heart made, finding failure in its scope.

V

As when a sick man very near to death
   Seems dead indeed, and feels begin and end
   The tears and takes the farewell of each friend,
And hears one bid the other go, draw breath
Freelier outside, ("since all is o'er," he saith,
   "And the blow fallen no grieving can amend;")   30

VI

While some discuss if near the other graves
   Be room enough for this, and when a day
   Suits best for carrying the corpse away,
With care about the banners, scarves and staves:
And still the man hears all, and only craves
   He may not shame such tender love and stay.

VII

Thus, I had so long suffered in this quest,
   Heard failure prophesied so oft, been writ
   So many times among "The Band"—to wit,
The knights who to the Dark Tower's search addressed   40
Their steps—that just to fail as they, seemed best,
   And all the doubt was now—should I be fit?

VIII

So, quiet as despair, I turned from him,
   That hateful cripple, out of his highway
   Into the path he pointed. All the day
Had been a dreary one at best, and dim
Was settling to its close, yet shot one grim
   Red leer to see the plain catch its estray.

IX

For mark! no sooner was I fairly found
   Pledged to the plain, after a pace or two,   50
   Than, pausing to throw backward a last view
O'er the safe road, 't was gone; grey plain all round:

48 estray the victim who has strayed

Nothing but plain to the horizon's bound.
I might go on; nought else remained to do.

X

So, on I went. I think I never saw
    Such starved ignoble nature; nothing throve:
    For flowers—as well expect a cedar grove!
But cockle, spurge, according to their law
Might propagate their kind, with none to awe,
60   You 'd think; a burr had been a treasure-trove.

XI

No! penury, inertness and grimace,
    In some strange sort, were the land's portion. "See
    "Or shut your eyes," said Nature peevishly,
"It nothing skills: I cannot help my case:
" 'T is the Last Judgment's fire must cure this place,
    "Calcine its clods and set my prisoners free."

XII

If there pushed any ragged thistle stalk
    Above its mates, the head was chopped; the bents
    Were jealous else. What made those holes and rents
70 In the dock's harsh swarth leaves, bruised as to balk
All hope of greenness? 't is a brute must walk
    Pashing their life out, with a brute's intents.

XIII

As for the grass, it grew as scant as hair
    In leprosy; thin dry blades pricked the mud
    Which underneath looked kneaded up with blood.
One stiff blind horse, his every bone a-stare,
Stood stupefied, however he came there:
    Thrust out past service from the devil's stud!

XIV

Alive? he might be dead for aught I know,
80   With that red gaunt and colloped neck a-strain,
    And shut eyes underneath the rusty mane;
Seldom went such grotesqueness with such woe;

66 **Calcine** turn to powder by means of heat   68 **bents** coarse grasses
80 **colloped** ridged

I never saw a brute I hated so;
   He must be wicked to deserve such pain.

XV

I shut my eyes and turned them on my heart.
   As a man calls for wine before he fights,
   I asked one draught of earlier, happier sights,
Ere fitly I could hope to play my part.
Think first, fight afterwards—the soldier's art:
   One taste of the old time sets all to rights.   90

XVI

Not it! I fancied Cuthbert's reddening face
   Beneath its garniture of curly gold,
   Dear fellow, till I almost felt him fold
An arm in mine to fix me to the place,
That way he used. Alas, one night's disgrace!
   Out went my heart's new fire and left it cold.

XVII

Giles then, the soul of honor—there he stands
   Frank as ten years ago when knighted first.
   What honest man should dare (he said) he durst.
Good—but the scene shifts—faugh! what hangman hands   100
Pin to his breast a parchment? His own bands
   Read it. Poor traitor, spit upon and curst!

XVIII

Better this present than a past like that;
   Back therefore to my darkening path again!
   No sound, no sight as far as eye could strain.
Will the night send a howlet or a bat?
I asked: when something on the dismal flat
   Came to arrest my thoughts and change their train.

XIX

A sudden little river crossed my path
   As unexpected as a serpent comes.   110
   No sluggish tide congenial to the glooms;
This, as it frothed by, might have been a bath
For the fiend's glowing hoof—to see the wrath
   Of its black eddy bespate with flakes and spumes.

114 **bespate** bespattered

XX

So petty yet so spiteful! All along,
 Low scrubby alders kneeled down over it;
 Drenched willows flung them headlong in a fit
Of mute despair, a suicidal throng:
The river which had done them all the wrong,
120 Whate'er that was, rolled by, deterred no whit.

XXI

Which, while I forded,—good saints, how I feared
 To set my foot upon a dead man's cheek,
 Each step, or feel the spear I thrust to seek
For hollows, tangled in his hair or beard!
 —It may have been a water rat I speared,
 But, ugh! it sounded like a baby's shriek.

XXII

Glad was I when I reached the other bank.
 Now for a better country. Vain presage!
 Who were the strugglers, what war did they wage,
130 Whose savage trample thus could pad the dank
Soil to a plash? Toads in a poisoned tank,
 Or wild cats in a red-hot iron cage—

XXIII

The fight must so have seemed in that fell cirque.
 What penned them there, with all the plain to choose?
No footprint leading to that horrid mews,
None out of it. Mad brewage set to work
Their brains, no doubt, like galley slaves the Turk
 Pits for his pastime, Christians against Jews.

XXIV

And more than that—a furlong on—why, there!
140 What bad use was that engine for, that wheel,
 Or brake, not wheel—that harrow fit to reel
Men's bodies out like silk? with all the air
Of Tophet's tool, on earth left unaware,
 Or brought to sharpen its rusty teeth of steel.

133 **cirque** arena   143 **Tophet** hell

XXV

Then came a bit of stubbed ground, once a wood,
  Next a marsh, it would seem, and now mere earth
  Desperate and done with; (so a fool finds mirth,
Makes a thing and then mars it, till his mood
Changes and off he goes!) within a rood—
  Bog, clay and rubble, sand and stark black dearth.   150

XXVI

Now blotches rankling, colored gay and grim,
  Now patches where some leanness of the soil's
  Broke into moss or substances like boils;
Then came some palsied oak, a cleft in him
Like a distorted mouth that splits its rim
  Gaping at death, and dies while it recoils.

XXVII

And just as far as ever from the end!
  Nought in the distance but the evening, nought
  To point my footstep further! At the thought,
A great black bird, Apollyon's bosom friend,   160
Sailed past, nor beat his wide wing dragon-penned
  That brushed my cap—perchance the guide I sought.

XXVIII

For, looking up, aware I somehow grew,
  'Spite of the dusk, the plain had given place
  All round to mountains—with such name to grace
Mere ugly heights and heaps now stolen in view.
How thus they had surprised me,—solve it, you!
  How to get from them was no clearer case.

XXIX

Yet half I seemed to recognize some trick
  Of mischief happened to me, God knows when—   170
  In a bad dream perhaps. Here ended, then,
Progress this way. When, in the very nick
Of giving up, one time more, came a click
  As when a trap shuts—you 're inside the den!

160 **Apollyon** a name for the devil. *See* Revelations IX:11. 161 **dragon-penned** with pinions like those of a dragon

XXX

Burningly it came on me all at once,
   This was the place! those two hills on the right,
   Crouched like two bulls locked horn in horn in fight;
While to the left, a tall scalped mountain . . . Dunce,
Dotard, a-dozing at the very nonce,
     After a life spent training for the sight!

180

XXXI

What in the midst lay but the Tower itself?
   The round squat turret, blind as the fool's heart,
   Built of brown stone, without a counterpart
In the whole world. The tempest's mocking elf
Points to the shipman thus the unseen shelf
     He strikes on, only when the timbers start.

XXXII

Not see? because of night perhaps?—why, day
   Came back again for that! before it left,
   The dying sunset kindled through a cleft:
The hills, like giants at a hunting, lay,
Chin upon hand, to see the game at bay,—
     "Now stab and end the creature—to the heft!"

190

XXXIII

Not hear? when noise was everywhere! it tolled
   Increasing like a bell. Names in my ears
   Of all the lost adventurers my peers,—
How such a one was strong, and such was bold,
And such was fortunate, yet each of old
     Lost, lost! one moment knelled the woe of years.

XXXIV

There they stood, ranged along the hillsides, met
   To view the last of me, a living frame
   For one more picture! in a sheet of flame
I saw them and I knew them all. And yet
Dauntless the slug-horn to my lips I set,
     And blew *"Childe Roland to the Dark Tower came."*

200

203 **slug-horn** a trumpet. There is actually no such horn; Browning was misled by Chatterton, who misunderstood the word *slogan,* a tribal battle-cry.

The Statue and the Bust

THERE 's a palace in Florence, the world knows well,
And a statue watches it from the square,
And this story of both do our townsmen tell.

Ages ago, a lady there,
At the farthest window facing the East
Asked, "Who rides by with the royal air?"

The bridesmaids' prattle around her ceased;
She leaned forth, one on either hand;
They saw how the blush of the bride increased—

They felt by its beats her heart expand—   10
As one at each ear and both in a breath
Whispered, "The Great-Duke Ferdinand."

That selfsame instant, underneath,
The Duke rode past in his idle way,
Empty and fine like a swordless sheath.

Gay he rode, with a friend as gay,
Till he threw his head back—"Who is she?"
—"A bride the Riccardi brings home today."

Hair in heaps lay heavily
Over a pale brow spirit-pure—   20
Carved like the heart of the coal-black tree,

Crisped like a war steed's encolure—
And vainly sought to dissemble her eyes
Of the blackest black our eyes endure.

And lo, a blade for a knight's emprise
Filled the fine empty sheath of a man,—
The Duke grew straightway brave and wise.

He looked at her, as a lover can;
She looked at him, as one who awakes:
The past was a sleep, and her life began.   30

22 **encolure** mane

Now, love so ordered for both their sakes,
A feast was held that selfsame night
In the pile which the mighty shadow makes.

(For Via Larga is three-parts light,
But the palace overshadows one,
Because of a crime which may God requite!

To Florence and God the wrong was done,
Through the first republic's murder there
By Cosimo and his cursed son.)

40   The Duke (with the statue's face in the square)
Turned in the midst of his multitude
At the bright approach of the bridal pair.

Face to face the lovers stood
A single minute and no more,
While the bridegroom bent as a man subdued—

Bowed till his bonnet brushed the floor—
For the Duke on the lady a kiss conferred,
As the courtly custom was of yore.

50   In a minute can lovers exchange a word?
If a word did pass, which I do not think,
Only one out of the thousand heard.

That was the bridegroom. At day's brink
He and his bride were alone at last
In a bedchamber by a taper's blink.

Calmly he said that her lot was cast,
That the door she had passed was shut on her
Till the final catafalk repassed.

The world meanwhile, its noise and stir,
Through a certain window facing the East,
60   She could watch like a convent's chronicler.

33 **the pile** the Grand-Duke's palace where the feast was held, built by Cosimo di Medici in 1430. The title of Grand-Duke was first assumed by Ferdinand, the man in the poem, in 1587.   57 **catafalk** a funeral carriage

Since passing the door might lead to a feast,
And a feast might lead to so much beside,
He, of many evils, chose the least.

"Freely I choose too," said the bride—
"Your window and its world suffice,"
Replied the tongue, while the heart replied—

"If I spend the night with that devil twice,
"May his window serve as my loop of hell
"Whence a damned soul looks on paradise!

"I fly to the Duke who loves me well,   70
"Sit by his side and laugh at sorrow
"Ere I count another ave-bell.

" 'T is only the coat of a page to borrow,
"And tie my hair in a horse-boy's trim,
"And I save my soul—but not tomorrow"—

(She checked herself and her eye grew dim)
"My father tarries to bless my state:
"I must keep it one day more for him.

"Is one day more so long to wait?
"Moreover the Duke rides past, I know;   80
"We shall see each other, sure as fate."

She turned on her side and slept. Just so!
So we resolve on a thing and sleep:
So did the lady, ages ago.

That night the Duke said, "Dear or cheap
"As the cost of this cup of bliss may prove
"To body or soul, I will drain it deep."

And on the morrow, bold with love,
He beckoned the bridegroom (close on call,
As his duty bade, by the Duke's alcove)   90

And smiled " 'T was a very funeral,
"Your lady will think, this feast of ours,—
"A shame to efface, whate'er befall!

72 **ave-bell** the bell for evening prayers

"What if we break from the Arno bowers,
"And try if Petraja, cool and green,
"Cure last night's fault with this morning's flowers?"

The bridegroom, not a thought to be seen
On his steady brow and quiet mouth,
Said, "Too much favor for me so mean!

100   "But, alas! my lady leaves the South;
"Each wind that comes from the Apennine
"Is a menace to her tender youth:

"Nor a way exists, the wise opine,
"If she quits her palace twice this year,
"To avert the flower of life's decline."

Quoth the Duke, "A sage and a kindly fear.
"Moreover Petraja is cold this spring:
"Be our feast tonight as usual here!"

And then to himself—"Which night shall bring
110   "Thy bride to her lover's embraces, fool—
"Or I am the fool, and thou art the king!

"Yet my passion must wait a night, nor cool—
"For tonight the Envoy arrives from France
"Whose heart I unlock with thyself, my tool.

"I need thee still and might miss perchance.
"Today is not wholly lost, beside,
"With its hope of my lady's countenance:

"For I ride—what should I do but ride?
"And passing her palace, if I list,
120   "May glance at its window—well betide!"

So said, so done: nor the lady missed
One ray that broke from the ardent brow,
Nor a curl of the lips where the spirit kissed.

Be sure that each renewed the vow,
No morrow's sun should arise and set
And leave them then as it left them now.

95 **Petraja** the Duke's villa, not far from Florence

But next day passed, and next day yet,
With still fresh cause to wait one day more
Ere each leaped over the parapet.

And still, as love's brief morning wore, 130
With a gentle start, half smile, half sigh,
They found love not as it seemed before.

They thought it would work infallibly,
But not in despite of heaven and earth:
The rose would blow when the storm passed by.

Meantime they could profit in winter's dearth
By store of fruits that supplant the rose:
The world and its ways have a certain worth:

And to press a point while these oppose
Were a simple policy; better wait: 140
We lose no friends and we gain no foes.

Meantime, worse fates than a lover's fate,
Who daily may ride and pass and look
Where his lady watches behind the grate!

And she—she watched the square like a book
Holding one picture and only one,
Which daily to find she undertook:

When the picture was reached the book was done,
And she turned from the picture at night to scheme
Of tearing it out for herself next sun. 150

So weeks grew months, years; gleam by gleam
The glory dropped from their youth and love,
And both perceived they had dreamed a dream;

Which hovered as dreams do, still above:
But who can take a dream for a truth?
Oh, hide our eyes from the next remove!

One day as the lady saw her youth
Depart, and the silver thread that streaked
Her hair, and, worn by the serpent's tooth,

159 serpent's tooth the ingratitude of her lover

160 The brow so puckered, the chin so peaked,—
And wondered who the woman was,
Hollow-eyed and haggard-cheeked,

Fronting her silent in the glass—
"Summon here," she suddenly said,
"Before the rest of my old self pass,

"Him, the Carver, a hand to aid,
"Who fashions the clay no love will change,
"And fixes a beauty never to fade.

170 "Let Robbia's craft so apt and strange
"Arrest the remains of young and fair,
"And rivet them while the seasons range.

"Make me a face on the window there,
"Waiting as ever, mute the while,
"My love to pass below in the square!

"And let me think that it may beguile
"Dreary days which the dead must spend
"Down in their darkness under the aisle,

"To say, 'What matters it at the end?
180 "'I did no more while my heart was warm
"'Than does that image, my pale-faced friend.'

"Where is the use of the lip's red charm,
"The heaven of hair, the pride of the brow,
"And the blood that blues the inside arm—

"Unless we turn, as the soul knows how,
"The earthly gift to an end divine?
"A lady of clay is as good, I trow."

But long ere Robbia's cornice, fine,
With flowers and fruits which leaves enlace,
Was set where now is the empty shrine—

169 **Robbia's craft** bas-relief in marble, bronze, or terra cotta, which the great della Robbias had brought to perfection. The ware was still made, though the last of the della Robbias had died in 1566.

(And, leaning out of a bright blue space,   190
As a ghost might lean from a chink of sky,
The passionate pale lady's face—

Eyeing ever, with earnest eye
And quick-turned neck at its breathless stretch,
Some one who ever is passing by—)

The Duke had sighed like the simplest wretch
In Florence, "Youth—my dream escapes!
"Will its record stay?" And he bade them fetch

Some subtle molder of brazen shapes—
"Can the soul, the will, die out of a man   200
"Ere his body find the grave that gapes?

"John of Douay shall effect my plan,
"Set me on horseback here aloft,
"Alive, as the crafty sculptor can,

"In the very square I have crossed so oft:
"That men may admire, when future suns
"Shall touch the eyes to a purpose soft,

"While the mouth and the brow stay brave in bronze—
"Admire and say, 'When he was alive
"'How he would take his pleasure once!'   210

"And it shall go hard but I contrive
"To listen the while, and laugh in my tomb
"At idleness which aspires to strive."

—————

So! While these wait the trump of doom,
How do their spirits pass, I wonder,
Nights and days in the narrow room?

Still, I suppose, they sit and ponder
What a gift life was, ages ago,
Six steps out of the chapel yonder.

202 **John of Douay** Giovanni da Bologna (1524-1608), who made the
equestrian statue of the Grand-Duke Ferdinand which stands in the
square

220
Only they see not God, I know,
Nor all that chivalry of his,
The soldier-saints who, row on row,

Burn upward each to his point of bliss—
Since, the end of life being manifest,
He had burned his way thro' the world to this.

I hear you reproach, "But delay was best,
"For their end was a crime."—Oh, a crime will do
As well, I reply, to serve for a test,

As a virtue golden through and through,
230
Sufficient to vindicate itself
And prove its worth at a moment's view!

Must a game be played for the sake of pelf?
Where a button goes, 't were an epigram
To offer the stamp of the very Guelph.

The true has no value beyond the sham:
As well the counter as coin, I submit,
When your table 's a hat, and your prize a dram.

Stake your counter as boldly every whit,
Venture as warily, use the same skill,
240
Do your best, whether winning or losing it,

If you choose to play!—is my principle.
Let a man contend to the uttermost
For his life's set prize, be it what it will!

The counter our lovers staked was lost
As surely as if it were lawful coin:
And the sin I impute to each frustrate ghost

Is—the unlit lamp and the ungirt loin,
Though the end in sight was a vice, I say.
You of the virtue (we issue join)
250
How strive you? *De te, fabula!*

234 **the stamp of the very Guelph** genuine coin. The Guelphs ruled Italy from the twelfth to the fifteenth centuries. 250 **De te, fabula** the fable concerns you

How It Strikes a Contemporary

I ONLY knew one poet in my life:
And this, or something like it, was his way.

You saw go up and down Valladolid,
A man of mark, to know next time you saw.
His very serviceable suit of black
Was courtly once and conscientious still,
And many might have worn it, though none did:
The cloak, that somewhat shone and showed the threads,
Had purpose, and the ruff, significance.
He walked and tapped the pavement with his cane,   10
Scenting the world, looking it full in face,
An old dog, bald and blindish, at his heels.
They turned up, now, the alley by the church,
That leads nowhither; now, they breathed themselves
On the main promenade just at the wrong time:
You 'd come upon his scrutinizing hat,
Making a peaked shade blacker than itself
Against the single window spared some house
Intact yet with its moldered Moorish work,—
Or else surprise the ferrel of his stick   20
Trying the mortar's temper 'tween the chinks
Of some new shop a-building, French and fine.
He stood and watched the cobbler at his trade,
The man who slices lemons into drink,
The coffee roaster's brazier, and the boys
That volunteer to help him turn its winch.
He glanced o'er books on stalls with half an eye,
And flyleaf ballads on the vendor's string,
And broad-edge bold-print posters by the wall.
He took such cognizance of men and things,   30
If any beat a horse, you felt he saw;
If any cursed a woman, he took note;
Yet stared at nobody,—you stared at him,
And found, less to your pleasure than surprise,
He seemed to know you and expect as much.

3 **Valladolid** a town in north-central Spain   19 **Moorish work** a survival
from the time when the Moors were masters of Spain   20 **ferrel** the iron
point of the cane   28 **flyleaf ballads** ballads printed on a single leaf of
paper

So, next time that a neighbor's tongue was loosed,
It marked the shameful and notorious fact,
We had among us, not so much a spy,
As a recording chief-inquisitor,
40   The town's true master if the town but knew!
We merely kept a governor for form,
While this man walked about and took account
Of all thought, said and acted, then went home,
And wrote it fully to our Lord the King
Who has an itch to know things, he knows why,
And reads them in his bedroom of a night.
Oh, you might smile! there wanted not a touch,
A tang of . . . well, it was not wholly ease
As back into your mind the man's look came.
50   Stricken in years a little,—such a brow
His eyes had to live under!—clear as flint
On either side the formidable nose
Curved, cut and colored like an eagle's claw.
Had he to do with A.'s surprising fate?
When altogether old B. disappeared
And young C. got his mistress,—was 't our friend,
His letter to the King, that did it all?
What paid the bloodless man for so much pains?
Our Lord the King has favorites manifold,
60   And shifts his ministry some once a month;
Our city gets new governors at whiles,—
But never word or sign, that I could hear,
Notified to this man about the streets
The King's approval of those letters conned
The last thing duly at the dead of night.
Did the man love his office? Frowned our Lord,
Exhorting when none heard—"Beseech me not!
"Too far above my people,—beneath me!
"I set the watch,—how should the people know?
70   "Forget them, keep me all the more in mind!"
Was some such understanding 'twixt the two?

    I found no truth in one report at least—
That if you tracked him to his home, down lanes
Beyond the Jewry, and as clean to pace,
You found he ate his supper in a room
Blazing with lights, four Titians on the wall,

44 **our Lord the King** God   74 **Jewry** the ghetto

And twenty naked girls to change his plate!
Poor man, he lived another kind of life
In that new stuccoed third house by the bridge,
Fresh-painted, rather smart than otherwise!   80
The whole street might o'erlook him as he sat,
Leg crossing leg, one foot on the dog's back,
Playing a decent cribbage with his maid
(Jacynth, you 're sure her name was) o'er the cheese
And fruit, three red halves of starved winter pears,
Or treat of radishes in April. Nine,
Ten, struck the church clock, straight to bed went he.

My father, like the man of sense he was,
Would point him out to me a dozen times;
"'St—'St," he 'd whisper, "the Corregidor!"   90
I had been used to think that personage
Was one with lacquered breeches, lustrous belt,
And feathers like a forest in his hat,
Who blew a trumpet and proclaimed the news,
Announced the bullfights, gave each church its turn,
And memorized the miracle in vogue!
He had a great observance from us boys;
We were in error; that was not the man.

I 'd like now, yet had haply been afraid,
To have just looked, when this man came to die,   100
And seen who lined the clean gay garret-sides
And stood about the neat low truckle-bed,
With the heavenly manner of relieving guard.
Here had been, mark, the general-in-chief,
Thro' a whole campaign of the world's life and death,
Doing the King's work all the dim day long,
In his old coat and up to knees in mud,
Smoked like a herring, dining on a crust,—
And, now the day was won, relieved at once!
No further show or need for that old coat,   110
You are sure, for one thing! Bless us, all the while
How sprucely we are dressed out, you and I!
A second, and the angels alter that.
Well, I could never write a verse,—could you?
Let 's to the Prado and make the most of time.

76 **Titians** paintings by the great Italian painter Titian (1477-1575) 90
Corregidor the chief magistrate 96 **memorized** celebrated 115 **Prado**
the promenade

Memorabilia

I

Aн, did you once see Shelley plain,
   And did he stop and speak to you
And did you speak to him again?
   How strange it seems and new!

II

But you were living before that,
   And also you are living after;
And the memory I started at—
   My starting moves your laughter.

III

I crossed a moor, with a name of its own
   And a certain use in the world no doubt,
Yet a hand's-breadth of it shines alone
   'Mid the blank miles round about:

IV

For there I picked up on the heather
   And there I put inside my breast
A molted feather, an eagle feather!
   Well, I forget the rest.

Andrea Del Sarto

CALLED "THE FAULTLESS PAINTER"

But do not let us quarrel any more,
No, my Lucrezia; bear with me for once:
Sit down and all shall happen as you wish.
You turn your face, but does it bring your heart?
I 'll work then for your friend's friend, never fear,

Title: things worth remembering   *Title:* Andrea d'Agnolo di Francisco di Luca (1486-1531) was the son of a Florentine tailor, and was therefore called "del Sarto." In writing this poem Browning had in mind Andrea's portraits of himself and his wife, painted late in the artist's life, and now hanging in the Pitti Palace in Florence.   **5 friend's friend** Lucrezia's "cousin"

Treat his own subject after his own way,
Fix his own time, accept too his own price,
And shut the money into this small hand
When next it takes mine. Will it? tenderly?
Oh, I 'll content him,—but tomorrow, Love!   10
I often am much wearier than you think,
This evening more than usual, and it seems
As if—forgive now—should you let me sit
Here by the window with your hand in mine
And look a half hour forth on Fiesole,
Both of one mind, as married people use,
Quietly, quietly the evening through,
I might get up tomorrow to my work
Cheerful and fresh as ever. Let us try.
Tomorrow, how you shall be glad for this!   20
Your soft hand is a woman of itself,
And mine the man's bared breast she curls inside.
Don't count the time lost, neither; you must serve   *they are not*
For each of the five pictures we require: *well off.*
It saves a model. So! keep looking so—
My serpentining beauty, rounds on rounds!
—How could you ever prick those perfect ears,
Even to put the pearl there! oh, so sweet—
My face, my moon, my everybody's moon,
Which everybody looks on and calls his,   30
And, I suppose, is looked on by in turn,
While she looks—no one's: very dear, no less.
You smile? why, there 's my picture ready made,
There 's what we painters call our harmony!
A common greyness silvers everything,—
All in a twilight, you and I alike
—You, at the point of your first pride in me
(That 's gone you know),—but I, at every point;
My youth, my hope, my art, being all toned down
To yonder sober pleasant Fiesole.   40
There 's the bell clinking from the chapel-top;
That length of convent wall across the way
Holds the trees safer, huddled more inside;
The last monk leaves the garden; days decrease,
And autumn grows, autumn in everything.
Eh? the whole seems to fall into a shape
As if I saw alike my work and self

15 **Fiesole** a suburb of Florence, on the hills to the east

And all that I was born to be and do,
A twilight-piece. Love, we are in God's hand.
50 How strange now, looks the life he makes us lead;
So free we seem, so fettered fast we are!
I feel he laid the fetter: let it lie!
This chamber for example—turn your head—
All that 's behind us! You don't understand
Nor care to understand about my art,
But you can hear at least when people speak:
And that cartoon, the second from the door
—It is the thing, Love! so such things should be—
Behold Madonna!—I am bold to say.
60 I can do with my pencil what I know,
What I see, what at bottom of my heart
I wish for, if I ever wish so deep—
Do easily, too—when I say, perfectly,
I do not boast, perhaps: yourself are judge,
Who listened to the Legate's talk last week,
And just as much they used to say in France.
At any rate 't is easy, all of it!
No sketches first, no studies, that 's long past:
I do what many dream of, all their lives,
70 —Dream? strive to do, and agonize to do,
And fail in doing. I could count twenty such
On twice your fingers, and not leave this town,
Who strive—you don't know how the others strive
To paint a little thing like that you smeared   *carelessness*
Carelessly passing with your robes afloat,—
Yet do much less, so much less, Someone says,
(I know his name, no matter)—so much less!
Well, less is more, Lucrezia: I am judged.
There burns a truer light of God in them,
80 In their vexed beating stuffed and stopped-up brain,
Heart, or whate'er else, than goes on to prompt
This low-pulsed forthright craftsman's hand of mine.
Their works drop groundward, but themselves, I know,
Reach many a time a heaven that 's shut to me,
Enter and take their place there sure enough,
Though they come back and cannot tell the world.
My works are nearer heaven, but I sit here.
The sudden blood of these men! at a word—

---

57 **cartoon** a preliminary drawing   65 **Legate** envoy of the Pope   76
Someone Michael Angelo   83 **drop groundward** are imperfect

Praise them, it boils, or blame them, it boils too.
I, painting from myself and to myself,   90
Know what I do, am unmoved by men's blame
Or their praise either. Somebody remarks
Morello's outline there is wrongly traced,
His hue mistaken; what of that? or else,
Rightly traced and well ordered; what of that?
Speak as they please, what does the mountain care?
Ah, but a man's reach should exceed his grasp,
Or what 's a heaven for? All is silver-grey
Placid and perfect with my art: the worse!
I know both what I want and what might gain,   100
And yet how profitless to know, to sigh
"Had I been two, another and myself,
"Our head would have o'erlooked the world!" No doubt.
Yonder 's a work now, of that famous youth
The Urbinate who died five years ago.
('T is copied, George Vasari sent it me.)
Well, I can fancy how he did it all,
Pouring his soul, with kings and popes to see,
Reaching, that heaven might so replenish him,
Above and through his art—for it gives way;   110
That arm is wrongly put—and there again—
A fault to pardon in the drawing's lines,
Its body, so to speak: its soul is right,
He means right—that, a child may understand.
Still, what an arm! and I could alter it:
But all the play, the insight and the stretch—
Out of me, out of me! And wherefore out?
Had you enjoined them on me, given me soul,
We might have risen to Rafael, I and you!
Nay, Love, you did give all I asked, I think—   120
More than I merit, yes, by many times.
But had you—oh, with the same perfect brow,
And perfect eyes, and more than perfect mouth,
And the low voice my soul hears, as a bird
The fowler's pipe, and follows to the snare—
Had you, with these the same, but brought a mind!
Some women do so. Had the mouth there urged
"God and the glory! never care for gain.

93 **Morello** a mountain north of Florence   105 **the Urbinate** Raphael,
born at Urbino   106 **Vasari** a pupil of Andrea's and author of the *Lives
of the Painters*

"The present by the future, what is that?
130   "Live for fame, side by side with Agnolo!
"Rafael is waiting: up to God, all three!"
I might have done it for you. So it seems:
Perhaps not. All is as God over-rules.
Beside, incentives come from the soul's self;
The rest avail not. Why do I need you?
What wife had Rafael, or has Agnolo?
In this world, who can do a thing, will not;
And who would do it, cannot, I perceive:
Yet the will 's somewhat—somewhat, too, the power—
140   And thus we half-men struggle. At the end,
God, I conclude, compensates, punishes.
'T is safer for me, if the award be strict,
That I am something underrated here,
Poor this long while, despised, to speak the truth.
I dared not, do you know, leave home all day,
For fear of chancing on the Paris lords.
The best is when they pass and look aside;
But they speak sometimes; I must bear it all.
Well may they speak! That Francis, that first time,
150   And that long festal year at Fontainebleau!
I surely then could sometimes leave the ground,
Put on the glory, Rafael's daily wear,
In that humane great monarch's golden look,—
One finger in his beard or twisted curl
Over his mouth's good mark that made the smile,
One arm about my shoulder, round my neck,
The jingle of his gold chain in my ear,
I painting proudly with his breath on me,
All his court round him, seeing with his eyes,
160   Such frank French eyes, and such a fire of souls
Profuse, my hand kept plying by those hearts,—
And, best of all, this, this, this face beyond,
This in the background, waiting on my work,
To crown the issue with a last reward!
A good time, was it not, my kingly days?
And had you not grown restless ... but I know—
'T is done and past; 't was right, my instinct said;
Too live the life grew, golden and not grey,
And I 'm the weak-eyed bat no sun should tempt

130 **Agnolo** Michael Angelo   149 **Francis** King Francis I of France,
Andrea's patron and benefactor

Out of the grange whose four walls make his world. 170
How could it end in any other way?
You called me, and I came home to your heart.
The triumph was—to reach and stay there; since
I reached it ere the triumph, what is lost?
Let my hands frame your face in your hair's gold,
You beautiful Lucrezia that are mine!
"Rafael did this, Andrea painted that;
"The Roman's is the better when you pray,
"But still the other's Virgin was his wife—"
Men will excuse me. I am glad to judge 180
Both pictures in your presence; clearer grows
My better fortune, I resolve to think.
For, do you know, Lucrezia, as God lives,
Said one day Agnolo, his very self,
To Rafael . . . I have known it all these years . . .
(When the young man was flaming out his thoughts
Upon a palace wall for Rome to see,
Too lifted up in heart because of it)
"Friend, there's a certain sorry little scrub
"Goes up and down our Florence, none cares how, 190
"Who, were he set to plan and execute
"As you are, pricked on by your popes and kings,
"Would bring the sweat into that brow of yours!"
To Rafael's!—And indeed the arm is wrong.
I hardly dare . . . yet, only you to see,
Give the chalk here—quick, thus the line should go!
Ay, but the soul! he's Rafael! rub it out!
Still, all I care for, if he spoke the truth,
(What he? why, who but Michel Agnolo?
Do you forget already words like those?) 200
If really there was such a chance, so lost,—
Is, whether you're—not grateful—but more pleased.
Well, let me think so. And you smile indeed!
This hour has been an hour! Another smile?
If you would sit thus by me every night
I should work better, do you comprehend?
I mean that I should earn more, give you more.
See, it is settled dusk now; there's a star;
Morello's gone, the watch lights show the wall,
The cue owls speak the name we call them by. 210
Come from the window, love,—come in, at last,

178 the Roman Raphael

Inside the melancholy little house
We built to be so gay with. God is just.
King Francis may forgive me: oft at nights
When I look up from painting, eyes tired out,
The walls become illumined, brick from brick
Distinct, instead of mortar, fierce bright gold,
That gold of his I did cement them with!
Let us but love each other. Must you go?
220 That Cousin here again? he waits outside?
Must see you—you, and not with me? Those loans?
More gaming debts to pay? you smiled for that?
Well, let smiles buy me! have you more to spend?
While hand and eye and something of a heart
Are left me, work 's my ware, and what 's it worth?
I 'll pay my fancy. Only let me sit
The grey remainder of the evening out,
Idle, you call it, and muse perfectly
How I could paint, were I but back in France,
230 One picture, just one more—the Virgin's face,
Not yours this time! I want you at my side
To hear them—that is, Michel Agnolo—
Judge all I do and tell you of its worth.
Will you? Tomorrow, satisfy your friend.
I take the subjects for his corridor,
Finish the portrait out of hand—there, there,
And throw him in another thing or two
If he demurs; the whole should prove enough
To pay for this same Cousin's freak. Beside,
240 What 's better and what 's all I care about,
Get you the thirteen scudi for the ruff!
Love, does that please you? Ah, but what does he,
The Cousin! what does he to please you more?

        I am grown peaceful as old age tonight.
I regret little, I would change still less.
Since there my past life lies, why alter it?
The very wrong to Francis!—it is true
I took his coin, was tempted and complied,
And built this house and sinned, and all is said.
250 My father and my mother died of want.
Well, had I riches of my own? you see

220 **Cousin** Lucrezia's lover   241 **scudi** a scudo was a coin, worth about
a dollar

How one gets rich! Let each one bear his lot.
They were born poor, lived poor, and poor they died:
And I have labored somewhat in my time
And not been paid profusely. Some good son
Paint my two hundred pictures—let him try!
No doubt, there 's something strikes a balance. Yes,
You loved me quite enough, it seems tonight.
This must suffice me here. What would one have?
In heaven, perhaps, new chances, one more chance— 260
Four great walls in the New Jerusalem,
Meted on each side by the angel's reed,
For Leonard, Rafael, Agnolo and me
To cover—the three first without a wife,
While I have mine! So—still they overcome
Because there 's still Lucrezia,—as I choose. *weak and foolish love*

Again the Cousin's whistle! Go, my Love.

"De Gustibus—"

I

YOUR ghost will walk, you lover of trees,
   (If our loves remain)
    In an English lane,
By a cornfield-side a-flutter with poppies.
Hark, those two in the hazel coppice—
A boy and a girl, if the good fates please,
    Making love, say,—
    The happier they!
Draw yourself up from the light of the moon,
And let them pass, as they will too soon, 10
    With the bean-flowers' boon,
    And the blackbird's tune,
    And May, and June!

II

What I love best in all the world
Is a castle, precipice-encurled,
In a gash of the wind-grieved Apennine.

263 **Leonard** Leonardo da Vinci *Title:* **"De gustibus non disputandum":**
There is no disputing about tastes

Or look for me, old fellow of mine,
(If I get my head from out the mouth
O' the grave, and loose my spirit's bands,
20   And come again to the land of lands)—
In a seaside house to the farther South,
Where the baked cicala dies of drouth,
And one sharp tree—'t is a cypress—stands,
By the many hundred years red-rusted,
Rough iron-spiked, ripe fruit-o'ercrusted,
My sentinel to guard the sands
To the water's edge. For, what expands
Before the house, but the great opaque
Blue breadth of sea without a break?
30   While, in the house, forever crumbles
Some fragment of the frescoed walls,
From blisters where a scorpion sprawls.
A girl bare-footed brings, and tumbles
Down on the pavement, green-flesh melons,
And says there 's news today—the king
Was shot at, touched in the liver-wing,
Goes with his Bourbon arm in a sling:
—She hopes they have not caught the felons.
Italy, my Italy!
40   Queen Mary's saying serves for me—
      (When fortune's malice
      Lost her—Calais)—
Open my heart and you will see
Graved inside of it, "Italy."
Such lovers old are I and she:
So it always was, so shall ever be!

35 **king** Ferdinand II, tyrant of the Two Sicilies 36 **liver-wing** right arm
40 **Queen Mary's saying** When the English lost Calais to the French in
1558, Mary Tudor, Queen of England, said that the name of Calais
would be found written on her heart after her death

Cleon

("As certain also of your own poets have said"—)

CLEON the poet (from the sprinkled isles,
Lily on lily, that o'erlace the sea,
And laugh their pride when the light wave lisps "Greece")—
To Protus in his Tyranny: much health!

They give thy letter to me, even now:
I read and seem as if I heard thee speak.
The master of thy galley still unlades
Gift after gift; they block my court at last
And pile themselves along its portico
Royal with sunset, like a thought of thee: 10
And one white she-slave from the group dispersed
Of black and white slaves (like the chequer-work
Pavement, at once my nation's work and gift,
Now covered with this settle-down of doves),
One lyric woman, in her crocus vest
Woven of sea-wools, with her two white hands
Commends to me the strainer and the cup
Thy lip hath bettered ere it blesses mine.

Well-counselled, king, in thy munificence!
For so shall men remark, in such an act   20
Of love for him whose song gives life its joy,
Thy recognition of the use of life;
Nor call thy spirit barely adequate
To help on life in straight ways, broad enough
For vulgar souls, by ruling and the rest.
Thou, in the daily building of thy tower,—
Whether in fierce and sudden spasms of toil,

Title: The characters of the poem are imaginary. The quotation at the head of the poem is from Paul's speech from the Areopagus in Athens; *See* Acts XVII:28. "For in him we live and move and have our being; as certain also of your own poets have said. For we are his offspring." The poet referred to is Aratus, a minor Greek poet. 1 **sprinkled isles** the Sporades, off the Greek coast 4 **Tyranny** a district or province under a tyrant. A tyrant was an absolute ruler, but the word did not carry the suggestion of oppression that it now does.

Or through dim lulls of unapparent growth,
Or when the general work 'mid good acclaim
30 Climbed with the eye to cheer the architect,—
Didst ne'er engage in work for mere work's sake—
Hadst ever in thy heart the luring hope
Of some eventual rest a-top of it,
Whence, all the tumult of the building hushed,
Thou first of men mightst look out to the East:
The vulgar saw thy tower, thou sawest the sun.
For this, I promise on thy festival
To pour libation, looking o'er the sea,
Making this slave narrate thy fortunes, speak
40 Thy great words, and describe thy royal face—
Wishing thee wholly where Zeus lives the most,
Within the eventual element of calm.

    Thy letter's first requirement meets me here.
It is as thou hast heard: in one short life
I, Cleon, have effected all those things
Thou wonderingly dost enumerate.
That epos on thy hundred plates of gold
Is mine,—and also mine the little chant,
So sure to rise from every fishing-bark
50 When, lights at prow, the seamen haul their net.
The image of the sun-god on the phare,
Men turn from the sun's self to see, is mine;
The Poecile, o'er-storied its whole length,
As thou didst hear, with painting, is mine too.
I know the true proportions of a man
And woman also, not observed before;
And I have written three books on the soul,
Proving absurd all written hitherto,
And putting us to ignorance again.
60 For music,—why, I have combined the moods,
Inventing one. In brief, all arts are mine;
Thus much the people know and recognize,
Throughout our seventeen islands. Marvel not.
We of these latter days, with greater mind

35 **the East** the source of light, and the home of Protus 43 **requirement** request 47 **epos** epic 51 **phare** lighthouse. The word comes from the island of Pharos, near Alexandria, where the Ptolemies established a great lighthouse. 53 **Poecile** the portico at Athens 60 **moods** modes in Greek music

Than our forerunners, since more composite,
Look not so great, beside their simple way,
To a judge who only sees one way at once,
One mind-point and no other at a time,—
Compares the small part of a man of us
With some whole man of the heroic age,   70
Great in his way—not ours, nor meant for ours.
And ours is greater, had we skill to know:
For, what we call this life of men on earth,
This sequence of the soul's achievements here
Being, as I find much reason to conceive,
Intended to be viewed eventually
As a great whole, not analyzed to parts,
But each part having reference to all,—
How shall a certain part, pronounced complete,
Endure effacement by another part?   80
Was the thing done?—then, what 's to do again?
See, in the chequered pavement opposite,
Suppose the artist made a perfect rhomb,
And next a lozenge, then a trapezoid—
He did not overlay them, superimpose
The new upon the old and blot it out,
But laid them on a level in his work,
Making at last a picture; there it lies.
So, first the perfect separate forms were made,
The portions of mankind; and after, so,   90
Occurred the combination of the same.
For where had been a progress, otherwise?
Mankind, made up of all the single men,—
In such a synthesis the labor ends.
Now mark me! those divine men of old time
Have reached, thou sayest well, each at one point
The outside verge that rounds our faculty;
And where they reach, who can do more than reach?
It takes but little water just to touch
At some one point the inside of a sphere,   100
And, as we turn the sphere, touch all the rest
In due succession: but the finer air
Which not so palpably nor obviously,
Though no less universally, can touch

83 **rhomb** a four-sided geometrical figure whose angles are not right
angles 84 **lozenge** a diamond-shaped rhomb **trapezoid** a four-sided
figure in which no sides, or only two sides, are parallel

The whole circumference of that emptied sphere,
Fills it more fully than the water did;
Holds thrice the weight of water in itself
Resolved into a subtler element.
And yet the vulgar call the sphere first full
110 Up to the visible height—and after, void;
Not knowing air's more hidden properties.
And thus our soul, misknown, cries out to Zeus
To vindicate his purpose in our life:
Why stay we on the earth unless to grow?
Long since, I imaged, wrote the fiction out,
That he or other god descended here
And, once for all, showed simultaneously
What, in its nature, never can be shown,
Piecemeal or in succession;—showed, I say,
120 The worth both absolute and relative
Of all his children from the birth of time,
His instruments for all appointed work.
I now go on to image,—might we hear
The judgment which should give the due to each,
Show where the labor lay and where the ease,
And prove Zeus' self, the latent everywhere!
This is a dream:—but no dream, let us hope,
That years and days, the summers and the springs,
Follow each other with unwaning powers.
130 The grapes which dye thy wine are richer far,
Through culture, than the wild wealth of the rock;
The suave plum than the savage-tasted drupe;
The pastured honeybee drops choicer sweet;
The flowers turn double, and the leaves turn flowers;
That young and tender crescent moon, thy slave,
Sleeping above her robe as buoyed by clouds,
Refines upon the women of my youth.
What, and the soul alone deteriorates?
I have not chanted verse like Homer, no—
140 Nor swept string like Terpander, no—nor carved
And painted men like Phidias and his friend:
I am not great as they are, point by point.

132 **drupe** any fruit in which the pulp encloses a stone   140 **Terpander** a musician and poet of Lesbos in the seventh century B.C.; the founder of Greek music   141 **Phidias** the great Greek sculptor of the fifth century B.C., who decorated the Parthenon **his friend** possibly Pericles (490?-429 B.C.), the ruler of Athens

But I have entered into sympathy
With these four, running these into one soul,
Who, separate, ignored each other's art.
Say, is it nothing that I know them all?
The wild flower was the larger; I have dashed
Rose-blood upon its petals, pricked its cup's
Honey with wine, and driven its seed to fruit,
And show a better flower if not so large: 150
I stand myself. Refer this to the gods
Whose gift alone it is! which, shall I dare
(All pride apart) upon the absurd pretext
That such a gift by chance lay in my hand,
Discourse of lightly or depreciate?
It might have fallen to another's hand: what then?
I pass too surely: let at least truth stay!

    And next, of what thou followest on to ask.
This being with me as I declare, O king,
My works, in all these varicolored kinds,   160
So done by me, accepted so by men—
Thou askest, if (my soul thus in men's hearts)
I must not be accounted to attain
The very crown and proper end of life?
Inquiring thence how, now life closeth up,
I face death with success in my right hand:
Whether I fear death less than dost thyself
The fortunate of men? "For" (writest thou)
"Thou leavest much behind, while I leave nought.
"Thy life stays in the poems men shall sing,   170
"The pictures men shall study; while my life,
"Complete and whole now in its power and joy,
"Dies altogether with my brain and arm,
"Is lost indeed; since, what survives myself?
"The brazen statue to o'erlook my grave,
"Set on the promontory which I named.
"And that—some supple courtier of my heir
"Shall use its robed and sceptred arm, perhaps,
"To fix the rope to, which best drags it down.
"I go then: triumph thou, who dost not go!"   180

    Nay, thou art worthy of hearing my whole mind.
Is this apparent, when thou turn'st to muse
Upon the scheme of earth and man in chief,

That admiration grows as knowledge grows?
That imperfection means perfection hid,
Reserved in part, to grace the aftertime?
If, in the morning of philosophy,
Ere aught had been recorded, nay perceived,
Thou, with the light now in thee, couldst have looked
190 On all earth's tenantry, from worm to bird,
Ere man, her last, appeared upon the stage—
Thou wouldst have seen them perfect, and deduced
The perfectness of others yet unseen.
Conceding which,—had Zeus then questioned thee
"Shall I go on a step, improve on this,
"Do more for visible creatures than is done?"
Thou wouldst have answered, "Ay, by making each
"Grow conscious in himself—by that alone.
"All 's perfect else: the shell sucks fast the rock,
200 "The fish strikes through the sea, the snake both swims
"And slides, forth range the beasts, the birds take flight,
"Till life's mechanics can no further go—
"And all this joy in natural life is put
"Like fire from off thy finger into each,
"So exquisitely perfect is the same.
"But 't is pure fire, and they mere matter are;
"It has them, not they it: and so I choose
"For man, thy last premeditated work
"(If I might add a glory to the scheme)
210 "That a third thing should stand apart from both,
"A quality arise within his soul,
"Which, introactive, made to supervise
"And feel the force it has, may view itself,
"And so be happy." Man might live at first
The animal life: but is there nothing more?
In due time, let him critically learn
How he lives; and, the more he gets to know
Of his own life's adaptabilities,
The more joy-giving will his life become.
220 Thus man, who hath this quality, is best.

But thou, king, hadst more reasonably said:
"Let progress end at once,—man make no step
"Beyond the natural man, the better beast,
"Using his senses, not the sense of sense."
In man there 's failure, only since he left

The lower and inconscious forms of life.
We called it an advance, the rendering plain
Man's spirit might grow conscious of man's life,
And, by new lore so added to the old,
Take each step higher over the brute's head.   230
This grew the only life, the pleasure-house,
Watchtower and treasure-fortress of the soul,
Which whole surrounding flats of natural life
Seemed only fit to yield subsistence to;
A tower that crowns a country. But alas,
The soul now climbs it just to perish there!
For thence we have discovered ('t is no dream—
We know this, which we had not else perceived)
That there 's a world of capability
For joy, spread round about it, meant for us,   240
Inviting us; and still the soul craves all,
And still the flesh replies, "Take no jot more
"Than ere thou clombst the tower to look abroad!
"Nay, so much less as that fatigue has brought
"Deduction to it." We struggle, fain to enlarge
Our bounded physical recipiency,
Increase our power, supply fresh oil to life,
Repair the waste of age and sickness: no,
It skills not! life 's inadequate to joy,
As the soul sees joy, tempting life to take.   250
They praise a fountain in my garden here
Wherein a Naiad sends the water-bow
Thin from her tube; she smiles to see it rise.
What if I told her, it is just a thread
From that great river which the hills shut up,
And mock her with my leave to take the same?
The artificer has given her one small tube
Past power to widen or exchange—what boots
To know she might spout oceans if she could?
She cannot lift beyond her first thin thread: 260
And so a man can use but a man's joy
While he sees God's. Is it for Zeus to boast,
"See, man, how happy I live, and despair—
"That I may be still happier—for thy use!"
If this were so, we could not thank our lord,
As hearts beat on to doing: 't is not so—
Malice it is not. Is it carelessness?

249 **skills not** is of no avail 252 **Naiad** water nymph

Still, no. If care—where is the sign? I ask,
And get no answer, and agree in sum,
270 O king, with thy profound discouragement,
Who seest the wider but to sigh the more.
Most progress is most failure: thou sayest well.

    The last point now:—thou dost except a case—
Holding joy not impossible to one
With artist gifts—to such a man as I
Who leave behind me living works indeed;
For, such a poem, such a painting lives.
What? dost thou verily trip upon a word,
Confound the accurate view of what joy is
280 (Caught somewhat clearer by my eyes than thine)
With feeling joy? confound the knowing how
And showing how to live (my faculty)
With actually living?—Otherwise
Where is the artist's vantage o'er the king?
Because in my great epos I display
How divers men young, strong, fair, wise, can act—
Is this as though I acted? if I paint,
Carve the young Phoebus, am I therefore young?
Methinks I'm older that I bowed myself
290 The many years of pain that taught me art!
Indeed, to know is something, and to prove
How all this beauty might be enjoyed, is more:
But, knowing nought, to enjoy is something too.
Yon rower, with the molded muscles there,
Lowering the sail, is nearer it than I.
I can write love odes: thy fair slave's an ode.
I get to sing of love, when grown too grey
For being beloved: she turns to that young man,
The muscles all a-ripple on his back.
300 I know the joy of kingship: well, thou art king!

    "But," sayest thou—(and I marvel, I repeat
To find thee trip on such a mere word) "what
"Thou writest, paintest, stays; that does not die:
"Sappho survives, because we sing her songs,
"And Aeschylus, because we read his plays!"
Why, if they live still, let them come and take

304 **Sappho** lyric poetess of Lesbos, born about 600 B.C.   305 **Aeschylus**
the earliest of the great Greek dramatists (525-426 B.C.)

Thy slave in my despite, drink from thy cup,
Speak in my place. Thou diest while I survive?
Say rather that my fate is deadlier still,
In this, that every day my sense of joy   310
Grows more acute, my soul (intensified
By power and insight) more enlarged, more keen;
While every day my hairs fall more and more,
My hand shakes, and the heavy years increase—
The horror quickening still from year to year,
The consummation coming past escape
When I shall know most, and yet least enjoy—
When all my works wherein I prove my worth,
Being present still to mock me in men's mouths,
Alive still, in the praise of such as thou,   320
I, I the feeling, thinking, acting man,
The man who loved his life so overmuch,
Sleep in my urn. It is so horrible,
I dare at times imagine to my need
Some future state revealed to us by Zeus,
Unlimited in capability
For joy, as this is in desire for joy,
—To seek which, the joy-hunger forces us:
That, stung by straitness of our life, made strait
On purpose to make prized the life at large—   330
Freed by the throbbing impulse we call death,
We burst there as the worm into the fly,
Who, while a worm still, wants his wings. But no!
Zeus has not yet revealed it; and alas,
He must have done so, were it possible!

Live long and happy, and in that thought die:
Glad for what was! Farewell. And for the rest,
I cannot tell thy messenger aright
Where to deliver what he bears of thine
To one called Paulus; we have heard his fame   340
Indeed, if Christus be not one with him—
I know not, nor am troubled much to know.
Thou canst not think a mere barbarian Jew
As Paulus proves to be, one circumcised,
Hath access to a secret shut from us?
Thou wrongest our philosophy, O king,

340 **Paulus** St. Paul, who began his European Mission about the year 50
A.D. and was in Athens soon after that date

In stooping to inquire of such an one,
As if his answer could impose at all!
He writeth, doth he? well, and he may write.
350   Oh, the Jew findeth scholars! certain slaves
Who touched on this same isle, preached him and Christ;
And (as I gathered from a bystander)
Their doctrine could be held by no sane man.

Two in the Campagna

I

I WONDER do you feel today
    As I have felt since, hand in hand,
We sat down on the grass, to stray
    In spirit better through the land,
This morn of Rome and May?

II

For me, I touched a thought, I know,
    Has tantalized me many times,
(Like turns of thread the spiders throw
    Mocking across our path) for rhymes
10   To catch at and let go.

III

Help me to hold it! First it left
    The yellowing fennel, run to seed
There, branching from the brickwork's cleft,
    Some old tomb's ruin: yonder weed
Took up the floating weft,

IV

Where one small orange cup amassed
    Five beetles,—blind and green they grope
Among the honey-meal: and last,
    Everywhere on the grassy slope
20   I traced it. Hold it fast!

Title: The campagna is the great open plain near Rome. It abounds in ruins of ancient Rome.

V

The champaign with its endless fleece
    Of feathery grasses everywhere!
Silence and passion, joy and peace,
    An everlasting wash of air—
Rome's ghost since her decease.

VI

Such life there, through such lengths of hours,
    Such miracles performed in play.
Such primal naked forms of flowers,
    Such letting nature have her way
While heaven looks from its towers!   30

VII

How say you? Let us, O my dove,
    Let us be unashamed of soul,
As earth lies bare to heaven above!
    How is it under our control
To love or not to love?

VIII

I would that you were all to me,
    You that are just so much, no more.
Nor yours nor mine, nor slave nor free!
    Where does the fault lie? What the core
O' the wound, since wound must be?   40

IX

I would I could adopt your will,
    See with your eyes, and set my heart
Beating by yours, and drink my fill
    At your soul's springs,—your part my part
In life, for good and ill.

X

No. I yearn upward, touch you close,
    Then stand away. I kiss your cheek,
Catch your soul's warmth,—I pluck the rose
    And love it more than tongue can speak—
Then the good minute goes.   50

XI

Already how am I so far
    Out of that minute? Must I go
Still like the thistle-ball, no bar,
    Onward, whenever light winds blow,
Fixed by no friendly star?

XII

Just when I seemed about to learn!
    Where is the thread now? Off again!
The old trick! Only I discern—
    Infinite passion, and the pain
60   Of finite hearts that yearn.

A Grammarian's Funeral

SHORTLY AFTER THE REVIVAL OF LEARNING IN EUROPE

LET us begin and carry up this corpse,
    Singing together.
Leave we the common crofts, the vulgar thorpes
    Each in its tether
Sleeping safe on the bosom of the plain,
    Cared-for till cock-crow:
Look out if yonder be not day again
    Rimming the rock-row!
That 's the appropriate country; there, man's thought,
10   Rarer, intenser,
Self-gathered for an outbreak, as it ought,
    Chafes in the censer.
Leave we the unlettered plain its herd and crop;
    Seek we sepulture
On a tall mountain, citied to the top,
    Crowded with culture!
All the peaks soar, but one the rest excels;
    Clouds overcome it;
No! yonder sparkle is the citadel's
20   Circling its summit.

3 **crofts** enclosed fields **thorpes** villages

Thither our path lies; wind we up the heights:
    Wait ye the warning?
Our low life was the level's and the night's;
    He 's for the morning.
Step to a tune, square chests, erect each head,
    'Ware the beholders!
This is our master, famous calm and dead,
    Borne on our shoulders.

Sleep, crop and herd! sleep, darkling thorpe and croft,
    Safe from the weather!   30
He, whom we convoy to his grave aloft,
    Singing together,
He was a man born with thy face and throat,
    Lyric Apollo!
Long he lived nameless: how should spring take note
    Winter would follow?
Till lo, the little touch, and youth was gone!
    Cramped and diminished,
Moaned he, "New measures, other feet anon!
    "My dance is finished?"   40
No, that 's the world's way: (keep the mountainside,
    Make for the city!)
He knew the signal, and stepped on with pride
    Over men's pity;
Left play for work, and grappled with the world
    Bent on escaping:
"What 's in the scroll," quoth he, "thou keepest furled?
    "Show me their shaping,
"Theirs who most studied man, the bard and sage,—
    "Give!"—So, he gowned him,   50
Straight got by heart that book to its last page:
    Learned, we found him.
Yea, but we found him bald too, eyes like lead,
    Accents uncertain:
"Time to taste life," another would have said,
    "Up with the curtain!"
This man said rather, "Actual life comes next?
    "Patience a moment!

34 **Apollo** the sun-god, renowned for his beauty and his music   47
scroll a roll of manuscript 50 **gowned him** became a scholar

"Grant I have mastered learning's crabbed text,
60   "Still there 's the comment.
"Let me know all! Prate not of most or least,
    "Painful or easy!
"Even to the crumbs I 'd fain eat up the feast,
    "Ay, nor feel queasy."
Oh, such a life as he resolved to live,
    When he had learned it,
When he had gathered all books had to give!
    Sooner, he spurned it.
Image the whole, then execute the parts—
70   Fancy the fabric
Quite, ere you build, ere steel strike fire from quartz,
    Ere mortar dab brick!

(Here 's the town gate reached: there 's the marketplace
    Gaping before us.)
Yea, this in him was the peculiar grace
    (Hearten our chorus!)
That before living he 'd learn how to live—
    No end to learning:
Earn the means first—God surely will contrive
80   Use for our earning.
Others mistrust and say, "But time escapes:
    "Live now or never!"
He said, "What 's time? leave Now for dogs and apes!
    "Man has Forever."
Back to his book then: deeper drooped his head:
    Calculus racked him:
Leaden before, his eyes grew dross of lead:
    Tussis attacked him.
"Now, master, take a little rest!"—not he!
90   (Caution redoubled,
Step two abreast, the way winds narrowly!)
    Not a whit troubled
Back to his studies, fresher than at first,
    Fierce as a dragon
He (soul-hydroptic with a sacred thirst)
    Sucked at the flagon.
Oh, if we draw a circle premature,
    Heedless of far gain,

86 **Calculus** gallstones   88 **Tussis** a bronchial cough   95 **soul-hydroptic**
thirsty of soul

Greedy for quick returns of profit, sure
    Bad is our bargain!   100
Was it not great? did not he throw on God,
    (He loves the burthen)—
God's task to make the heavenly period
    Perfect the earthen?
Did not he magnify the mind, show clear
    Just what it all meant?
He would not discount life, as fools do here,
    Paid by instalment!
He ventured neck or nothing—heaven's success
    Found, or earth's failure: 110
"Wilt thou trust death or not?" He answered "Yes:
    "Hence with life's pale lure!"
That low man seeks a little thing to do,
    Sees it and does it:
This high man, with a great thing to pursue,
    Dies ere he knows it.
That low man goes on adding one to one,
    His hundred 's soon hit:
This high man, aiming at a million,
    Misses an unit.   120
That, has the world here—should he need the next,
    Let the world mind him!
This, throws himself on God, and unperplexed
    Seeking shall find him.
So, with the throttling hands of death at strife,
    Ground he at grammar;
Still, thro' the rattle, parts of speech were rife:
    While he could stammer
He settled *Hoti's* business—let it be!—
    Properly based *Oun*—   130
Give us the doctrine of the enclitic *De,*
    Dead from the waist down.
Well, here 's the platform, here 's the proper place:
    Hail to your purlieus,
All ye highfliers of the feathered race,
    Swallows and curlews!
Here 's the top peak; the multitude below
    Live, for they can, there:

127 **rattle** the death rattle 129-31 **Hoti ... Oun ... De** Greek particles, meaning respectively "that," "therefore," "towards"

This man decided not to Live but Know—
140   Bury this man there?
Here—here 's his place, where meteors shoot, clouds form,
    Lightnings are loosened,
Stars come and go! Let joy break with the storm,
    Peace let the dew send!
Lofty designs must close in like effects:
    Loftily lying,
Leave him—still loftier than the world suspects,
    Living and dying.

One Word More

TO E. B. B.

1855

I

THERE they are, my fifty men and women
Naming me the fifty poems finished!
Take them, Love, the book and me together:
Where the heart lies, let the brain lie also.

II

Rafael made a century of sonnets,
Made and wrote them in a certain volume
Dinted with the silver-pointed pencil
Else he only used to draw Madonnas:
These, the world might view—but one, the volume.
10 Who that one, you ask? Your heart instructs you.
Did she live and love it all her lifetime?

Title: This poem dedicated the volume *Men and Women,* consisting of fifty poems and published in 1855, to Browning's wife, Elizabeth Barrett Browning 5 **Rafael** the painter (1483-1520). Browning follows the story, begun by Vasari, that Raphael wrote a century of sonnets to La Fornacina, the young woman who served as model for his pictures of the Madonna. The tradition is apocryphal, for only three and a part of a fourth sonnet by Raphael are extant, and the book which Guido Reni treasured (ll. 27-31) was a book of original designs by the painter.

Did she drop, his lady of the sonnets,
Die, and let it drop beside her pillow
Where it lay in place of Rafael's glory,
Rafael's cheek so duteous and so loving—
Cheek, the world was wont to hail a painter's,
Rafael's cheek, her love had turned a poet's?

III

You and I would rather read that volume,
(Taken to his beating bosom by it)
Lean and list the bosom-beats of Rafael,   20
Would we not? than wonder at Madonnas—
Her, San Sisto names, and Her, Foligno,
Her, that visits Florence in a vision,
Her, that 's left with lilies in the Louvre—
Seen by us and all the world in circle.

IV

You and I will never read that volume.
Guido Reni, like his own eye's apple
Guarded long the treasure-book and loved it.
Guido Reni dying, all Bologna
Cried, and the world cried too, "Ours, the treasure!"   30
Suddenly, as rare things will, it vanished.

V

Dante once prepared to paint an angel:
Whom to please? You whisper "Beatrice."
While he mused and traced it and retraced it,
(Peradventure with a pen corroded
Still by drops of that hot ink he dipped for,
When, his left hand i' the hair o' the wicked,
Back he held the brow and pricked its stigma,

---

22 **San Sisto** the Sistine Madonna in Dresden. **Foligno** the Madonna of
Foligno is at Rome   23 **Florence** the Madonna del Granduca is in the
Pitti Palace in Florence   24 **Louvre** the Madonna of the Garden is in the
Louvre in Paris   32 **Dante** Browning in this section is following Boccaccio
in a well-authenticated legend, but making his own interpretation of the
event. *See* Dante's *Vita Nuova*, Ch. 35 ff.   35 **pen corroded** by the fierce
writing of Dante in the *Inferno;* but it is unlikely that the *Inferno* was
begun as early as 1291, when the incident referred to took place

Bit into the live man's flesh for parchment,
40   Loosed him, laughed to see the writing rankle,
Let the wretch go festering through Florence)—
Dante, who loved well because he hated,
Hated wickedness that hinders loving,
Dante standing, studying his angel,—
In there broke the folk of his Inferno.
Says he—"Certain people of importance"
(Such he gave his daily dreadful line to)
"Entered and would seize, forsooth, the poet."
Says the poet—"Then I stopped my painting."

VI

50   You and I would rather see that angel,
Painted by the tenderness of Dante,
Would we not?—than read a fresh Inferno.

VII

You and I will never see that picture.
While he mused on love and Beatrice,
While he softened o'er his outlined angel,
In they broke, those "people of importance":
We and Bice bear the loss for ever.

VIII

What of Rafael's sonnets, Dante's picture?
This: no artist lives and loves, that longs not
60   Once, and only once, and for one only,
(Ah, the prize!) to find his love a language
Fit and fair and simple and sufficient—
Using nature that 's an art to others,
Not, this one time, art that 's turned his nature.
Ay, of all the artists living, loving,
None but would forego his proper dowry,—
Does he paint? he fain would write a poem,—
Does he write? he fain would paint a picture,
Put to proof art alien to the artist's,
70   Once, and only once, and for one only,

39 **live man's flesh** Dante portrayed living men as if they were already
dead and in hell   48 **seize** there is no indication in the *Vita Nuova* that
these people came to do Dante harm   54 **Beatrice** Beatrice Portinari,
called "Bice" for short, was the lady beloved by Dante

So to be the man and leave the artist,
Gain the man's joy, miss the artist's sorrow.

IX

Wherefore? Heaven's gift takes earth's abatement!
He who smites the rock and spreads the water,
Bidding drink and live a crowd beneath him,
Even he, the minute makes immortal,
Proves, perchance, but mortal in the minute,
Desecrates, belike, the deed in doing.
While he smites, how can he but remember,
So he smote before, in such a peril,   80
When they stood and mocked—"Shall smiting help us?"
When they drank and sneered—"A stroke is easy!"
When they wiped their mouths and went their journey,
Throwing him for thanks—"But drought was pleasant."
Thus old memories mar the actual triumph;
Thus the doing savors of disrelish;
Thus achievement lacks a gracious somewhat;
O'er-importuned brows becloud the mandate,
Carelessness or consciousness, the gesture.
For he bears an ancient wrong about him,   90
Sees and knows again those phalanxed faces,
Hears, yet one time more, the 'customed prelude—
"How shouldst thou, of all men, smite, and save us?"
Guesses what is like to prove the sequel—
"Egypt's fleshpots—nay, the drought was better."

X

Oh, the crowd must have emphatic warrant!
Theirs, the Sinai-forehead's cloven brilliance,
Right-arm's rod-sweep, tongue's imperial fiat.
Never dares the man put off the prophet.

XI

Did he love one face from out the thousands,   100
(Were she Jethro's daughter, white and wifely,
Were she but the Aethiopian bondslave,)

74 **He who smites the rock** Moses. *See* Exodus XVI-XIX, and Numbers
XII and XX. 95 **Egypt's fleshpots** *See* Exodus XVI:3. The Israelites in
Egypt ate and drank to the full. 97 **Sinai** God appeared on Mt. Sinai in
lightning and thunder. *See* Exodus XIX. 101-2 **Jethro's daughter** Zip-
porah, wife of Moses. Moses also married an Ethiopian woman of low
degree.

He would envy yon dumb patient camel,
Keeping a reserve of scanty water
Meant to save his own life in the desert;
Ready in the desert to deliver
(Kneeling down to let his breast be opened)
Hoard and life together for his mistress.

XII

I shall never, in the years remaining,
Paint you pictures, no, nor carve you statues,
Make you music that should all-express me;
So it seems: I stand on my attainment.
This of verse alone, one life allows me;
Verse and nothing else have I to give you.
Other heights in other lives, God willing:
All the gifts from all the heights, your own; Love!

XIII

Yet a semblance of resource avails us—
Shade so finely touched, love's sense must seize it.
Take these lines, look lovingly and nearly,
Lines I write the first time and the last time.
He who works in fresco, steals a hair-brush,
Curbs the liberal hand, subservient proudly,
Cramps his spirit, crowds its all in little,
Makes a strange art of an art familiar,
Fills his lady's missal-marge with flowerets.
He who blows thro' bronze, may breathe thro' silver,
Fitly serenade a slumbrous princess.
He who writes, may write for once as I do.

XIV

Love, you saw me gather men and women,
Live or dead or fashioned by my fancy,
Enter each and all, and use their service,
Speak from every mouth,—the speech, a poem.
Hardly shall I tell my joys and sorrows,
Hopes and fears, belief and disbelieving:
I am mine and yours—the rest be all men's,
Karshish, Cleon, Norbert and the fifty.
Let me speak this once in my true person,
Not as Lippo, Roland or Andrea,
Though the fruit of speech be just this sentence:

110

120

130

Pray you, look on these my men and women,   140
Take and keep my fifty poems finished;
Where my heart lies, let my brain lie also!
Poor the speech; be how I speak, for all things.

XV

Not but that you know me! Lo, the moon's self!
Here in London, yonder late in Florence,
Still we find her face, the thrice-transfigured.
Curving on a sky imbrued with color,
Drifted over Fiesole by twilight,
Came she, our new crescent of a hair's-breadth.
Full she flared it, lamping Samminiato,   150
Rounder 'twixt the cypresses and rounder,
Perfect till the nightingales applauded.
Now, a piece of her old self, impoverished,
Hard to greet, she traverses the houseroofs,
Hurries with unhandsome thrift of silver,
Goes dispiritedly, glad to finish.

XVI

What, there's nothing in the moon noteworthy?
Nay: for if that moon could love a mortal,
Use, to charm him (so to fit a fancy),
All her magic ('t is the old sweet mythos)   160
She would turn a new side to her mortal,
Side unseen of herdsman, huntsman, steersman—
Blank to Zoroaster on his terrace,
Blind to Galileo on his turret,
Dumb to Homer, dumb to Keats—him, even!
Think, the wonder of the moonstruck mortal—
When she turns round, comes again in heaven,
Opens out anew for worse or better!
Proves she like some portent of an iceberg
Swimming full upon the ship it founders,   170
Hungry with huge teeth of splintered crystals?
Proves she as the paved work of a sapphire
Seen by Moses when he climbed the mountain?

146 **thrice-transfigured** the new, full, and waning moon   148 **Fiesole** a
town east of Florence   160 **mythos** the legend of Diana's love for Endymion   163 **Zoroaster** the founder of the religion of Iran, in which the
chief quality of God was light, and therefore the heavenly bodies were
worshipped   164 **Galileo** the great Italian astronomer (1564-1642)   165
Keats John Keats, author of *Endymion*

Moses, Aaron, Nadab and Abihu
Climbed and saw the very God, the Highest,
Stand upon the paved work of a sapphire.
Like the bodied heaven in his clearness
Shone the stone, the sapphire of that paved work,
When they ate and drank and saw God also!

XVII

180   What were seen? None knows, none ever shall know.
Only this is sure—the sight were other,
Not the moon's same side, born late in Florence,
Dying now impoverished here in London.
God be thanked, the meanest of his creatures
Boasts two soul-sides, one to face the world with,
One to show a woman when he loves her!

XVIII

This I say of me, but think of you, Love!
This to you—yourself my moon of poets!
Ah, but that 's the world's side, there 's the wonder,
190   Thus they see you, praise you, think they know you!
There, in turn I stand with them and praise you—
Out of my own self, I dare to phrase it.
But the best is when I glide from out them,
Cross a step or two of dubious twilight,
Come out on the other side, the novel
Silent silver lights and darks undreamed of,
Where I hush and bless myself with silence.

XIX

Oh, their Rafael of the dear Madonnas,
Oh, their Dante of the dread Inferno,
200   Wrote one song—and in my brain I sing it,
Drew one angel—borne, see, on my bosom!

174 **Moses, Aaron, Nadab and Abihu** *See* Exodus xxiv:9-10

Abt Vogler

AFTER HE HAS BEEN EXTEMPORIZING UPON THE
MUSICAL INSTRUMENT OF HIS INVENTION

I

Would that the structure brave, the manifold music I build,
  Bidding my organ obey, calling its keys to their work,
Claiming each slave of the sound, at a touch, as when Solomon
    willed
Armies of angels that soar, legions of demons that lurk,
Man, brute, reptile, fly,—alien of end and of aim,
  Adverse, each from the other heaven-high, hell-deep re-
    moved,—
Should rush into sight at once as he named the ineffable Name,
  And pile him a palace straight, to pleasure the princess he
    loved!

II

Would it might tarry like his, the beautiful building of mine,
  This which my keys in a crowd pressed and importuned
    to raise!   10
Ah, one and all, how they helped, would dispart now and now
    combine,
  Zealous to hasten the work, heighten their master his praise!
And one would bury his brow with a blind plunge down to
    hell,
  Burrow awhile and build, broad on the roots of things,
Then up again swim into sight, having based me my palace
    well,
  Founded it, fearless of flame, flat on the nether springs.

III

And another would mount and march, like the excellent
  minion he was,

Title: Abbé Georg Joseph Vogler (1749-1814) was a German musician
who was very devout, and a notable improviser. He taught Weber, Meyer-
beer, and Browning's own music master, John Relfe. Vogler was inventive,
and the musical instrument which he designed and used was a small port-
able organ called an orchestrion. 3 Solomon according to Talmudic
legend Solomon had a seal with the "ineffable Name" of God upon it; by
this seal he had power over supernatural beings. The building of Solomon's palace took thirteen years. 11 dispart separate 17 minion servant

Ay, another and yet another, one crowd but with many a
        crest,
Raising my rampired walls of gold as transparent as glass,
20   Eager to do and die, yield each his place to the rest:
For higher still and higher (as a runner tips with fire,
        When a great illumination surprises a festal night—
Outlining round and round Rome's dome from space to spire)
        Up, the pinnacled glory reached, and the pride of my soul
        was in sight.

IV

In sight? Not half! for it seemed, it was certain, to match
        man's birth,
        Nature in turn conceived, obeying an impulse as I;
And the emulous heaven yearned down, made effort to reach
        the earth,
        As the earth had done her best, in my passion, to scale the
        sky:
Novel splendors burst forth, grew familiar and dwelt with
        mine,
30   Not a point nor peak but found and fixed its wandering star;
Meteor-moons, balls of blaze: and they did not pale nor pine,
        For earth had attained to heaven, there was no more near
        nor far.

V

Nay more; for there wanted not who walked in the glare and
        glow,
        Presences plain in the place; or, fresh from the Protoplast,
Furnished for ages to come, when a kindlier wind should
        blow,
        Lured now to begin and live, in a house to their liking at
        last;
Or else the wonderful Dead who have passed through the
        body and gone,
        But were back once more to breathe in an old world worth
        their new:
What never had been, was now; what was, as it shall be anon;
        And what is,—shall I say, matched both? for I was made
40   perfect too.

19 **rampired walls** walls with ramparts   34 **Protoplast** first created, first
life-substance

VI

All through my keys that gave their sounds to a wish of my
  soul,
  All through my soul that praised as its wish flowed visibly
  forth,
All through music and me! For think, had I painted the
  whole,
  Why, there it had stood, to see, nor the process so wonder-
  worth:
Had I written the same, made verse—still, effect proceeds
  from cause,
  Ye know why the forms are fair, ye hear how the tale is told;
It is all triumphant art, but art in obedience to laws,
  Painter and poet are proud in the artist-list enrolled:—

VII

But here is the finger of God, a flash of the will that can,
  Existent behind all laws, that made them and, lo, they are! 50
And I know not if, save in this, such gift be allowed to man,
  That out of three sounds he frame, not a fourth sound, but
  a star.
Consider it well: each tone of our scale in itself is nought;
  It is everywhere in the world—loud, soft, and all is said:
Give it to me to use! I mix it with two in my thought:
  And, there! Ye have heard and seen: consider and bow the
  head!

VIII

Well, it is gone at last, the palace of music I reared;
  Gone! and the good tears start, the praises that come too
  slow;
For one is assured at first, one scarce can say that he feared,
  That he even gave it a thought, the gone thing was to go. 60
Never to be again! But many more of the kind
  As good, nay, better perchance: is this your comfort to me?
To me, who must be saved because I cling with my mind
  To the same, same self, same love, same God: ay, what was,
  shall be.

IX

Therefore to whom turn I but to thee, the ineffable Name?
  Builder and maker, thou, of houses not made with hands!

49 **the will that can** the creative will   66 **houses not made with hands**
See II Corinthians v:1

What, have fear of change from thee who art ever the same?
　Doubt that thy power can fill the heart that thy power
　　expands?
There shall never be one lost good! What was, shall live as
　before;
70　The evil is null, is nought, is silence implying sound;
What was good shall be good, with, for evil, so much good
　more;
　On the earth the broken arcs; in the heaven, a perfect round.

X

All we have willed or hoped or dreamed of good shall exist;
　Not its semblance, but itself; no beauty, nor good, nor power
Whose voice has gone forth, but each survives for the melodist
　When eternity affirms the conception of an hour.
The high that proved too high, the heroic for earth too hard,
　The passion that left the ground to lose itself in the sky,
Are music sent up to God by the lover and the bard;
80　Enough that he heard it once: we shall hear it by-and-by.

XI

And what is our failure here but a triumph's evidence
　For the fulness of the days? Have we withered or agonized?
Why else was the pause prolonged but that singing might
　issue thence?
　Why rushed the discords in but that harmony should be
　　prized?
Sorrow is hard to bear, and doubt is slow to clear,
　Each sufferer says his say, his scheme of the weal and woe:
But God has a few of us whom he whispers in the ear;
　The rest may reason and welcome: 't is we musicians know.

XII

Well, it is earth with me; silence resumes her reign:
90　I will be patient and proud, and soberly acquiesce.
Give me the keys. I feel for the common chord again,
　Sliding by semitones, till I sink to the minor,—yes,
And I blunt it into a ninth, and I stand on alien ground,
　Surveying awhile the heights I rolled from into the deep;
Which, hark, I have dared and done, for my resting place is
　found,
　The C Major of this life: so, now I will try to sleep.
91 **common chord** the fundamental tone; the common level of life

Rabbi Ben Ezra

I

Grow old along with me!
  The best is yet to be,
The last of life, for which the first was made:
  Our times are in His hand
  Who saith "A whole I planned,
"Youth shows but half; trust God: see all nor be afraid!"

II

Not that, amassing flowers,
  Youth sighed "Which rose make ours,
"Which lily leave and then as best recall?"
  Not that, admiring stars,
  It yearned "Nor Jove, nor Mars;   10
"Mine be some figured flame which blends, transcends them
      all!"

III

Not for such hopes and fears
  Annulling youth's brief years,
Do I remonstrate: folly wide the mark!
  Rather I prize the doubt
  Low kinds exist without,
Finished and finite clods, untroubled by a spark.

IV

Poor vaunt of life indeed,
  Were man but formed to feed   20
On joy, to solely seek and find and feast:
  Such feasting ended, then
  As sure an end to men;
Irks care the crop-full bird? Frets doubt the maw-crammed
      beast?

Title: Abraham Ibn Ezra was a Spanish rabbi of the twelfth century. He
travelled widely in the latter part of his life, and was renowned for his
learning. His *Commentary on Isaiah* was probably known to Browning.
The sentiments of the poem are Browning's, and the poem may have been
written in answer to FitzGerald's *Rubáiyát of Omar Khayyám.* **12 figured**
imagined

V

Rejoice we are allied
To That which doth provide
And not partake, effect and not receive!
 A spark disturbs our clod;
 Nearer we hold of God
30 Who gives, than of His tribes that take, I must believe.

VI

Then, welcome each rebuff
That turns earth's smoothness rough,
Each sting that bids nor sit nor stand but go!
 Be our joys three-parts pain!
 Strive, and hold cheap the strain;
Learn, nor account the pang; dare, never grudge the throe!

VII

For thence,—a paradox
Which comforts while it mocks,—
Shall life succeed in that it seems to fail:
40 What I aspired to be,
 And was not, comforts me:
A brute I might have been, but would not sink i' the scale.

VIII

What is he but a brute
Whose flesh has soul to suit,
Whose spirit works lest arms and legs want play?
 To man, propose this test—
 Thy body at its best,
How far can that project thy soul on its lone way?

IX

Yet gifts should prove their use:
50 I own the Past profuse
Of power each side, perfection every turn:
 Eyes, ears took in their dole,
 Brain treasured up the whole;
Should not the heart beat once "How good to live and learn?"

42 **scale** the scale of being

X

Not once beat "Praise be Thine!
    "I see the whole design,
"I, who saw power, see now love perfect too:
    "Perfect I call Thy plan:
    "Thanks that I was a man!
"Maker, remake, complete,—I trust what Thou shalt do!"   60

XI

For pleasant is this flesh;
    Our soul, in its rose-mesh
Pulled ever to the earth, still yearns for rest;
    Would we some prize might hold
    To match those manifold
Possessions of the brute,—gain most, as we did best!

XII

Let us not always say
    "Spite of this flesh today
"I strove, made head, gained ground upon the whole!"
    As the bird wings and sings,   70
    Let us cry "All good things
"Are ours, for soul helps flesh more, now, than flesh helps
    soul!"

XIII

Therefore I summon age
    To grant youth's heritage,
Life's struggle having so far reached its term:
    Thence shall I pass, approved
    A man, for aye removed
From the developed brute; a god though in the germ.

XIV

And I shall thereupon
    Take rest, ere I be gone   80
Once more on my adventure brave and new:
    Fearless and unperplexed,
    When I wage battle next,
What weapons to select, what armor to indue.

75 term limit **81 adventure brave and new** in the life beyond the grave

XV

Youth ended, I shall try
My gain or loss thereby;
Leave the fire ashes, what survives is gold:
And I shall weigh the same,
Give life its praise or blame:
90 Young, all lay in dispute; I shall know, being old.

XVI

For note, when evening shuts,
A certain moment cuts
The deed off, calls the glory from the grey:
A whisper from the west
Shoots—"Add this to the rest,
"Take it and try its worth: here dies another day."

XVII

So, still within this life,
Though lifted o'er its strife,
Let me discern, compare, pronounce at last,
100   "This rage was right i' the main,
That acquiescence vain:
"The Future I may face now I have proved the Past."

XVIII

For more is not reserved
To man, with soul just nerved
To act tomorrow what he learns today:
Here, work enough to watch
The Master work, and catch
Hints of the proper craft, tricks of the tool's true play.

XIX

As it was better, youth
110   Should strive, through acts uncouth,
Toward making, than repose on aught found made:
So, better, age, exempt
From strife, should know, than tempt
Further. Thou waitedest age: wait death nor be afraid!

XX

Enough now, if the Right
    And Good and Infinite
Be named here, as thou callest thy hand thine own,
    With knowledge absolute,
    Subject to no dispute
From fools that crowded youth, nor let thee feel alone.   120

XXI

Be there, for once and all,
    Severed great minds from small,
Announced to each his station in the Past!
    Was I, the world arraigned,
    Were they, my soul disdained,
Right? Let age speak the truth and give us peace at last!

XXII

Now, who shall arbitrate?
    Ten men love what I hate,
Shun what I follow, slight what I receive;
    Ten, who in ears and eyes   130
    Match me: we all surmise,
They this thing, and I that: whom shall my soul believe?

XXIII

Not on the vulgar mass
    Called "work," must sentence pass,
Things done, that took the eye and had the price;
    O'er which, from level stand,
    The low world laid its hand,
Found straightway to its mind, could value in a trice:

XXIV

But all, the world's coarse thumb
    And finger failed to plumb,   140
So passed in making up the main account;
    All instincts immature,
    All purposes unsure,
That weighed not as his work, yet swelled the man's amount:

141 **passed** passed by, neglected

XXV

Thoughts hardly to be packed
Into a narrow act,
Fancies that broke through language and escaped;
All I could never be,
All, men ignored in me,
150 This, I was worth to God, whose wheel the pitcher shaped.

XXVI

Ay, note that Potter's wheel,
That metaphor! and feel
Why time spins fast, why passive lies our clay,—
Thou, to whom fools propound,
When the wine makes its round,
"Since life fleets, all is change; the Past gone, seize today!"

XXVII

Fool! All that is, at all,
Lasts ever, past recall;
Earth changes, but thy soul and God stand sure:
160 What entered into thee,
That was, is, and shall be:
Time's wheel runs back or stops: Potter and clay endure.

XXVIII

He fixed thee mid this dance
Of plastic circumstance,
This Present, thou, forsooth, wouldst fain arrest:
Machinery just meant
To give thy soul its bent,
Try thee and turn thee forth, sufficiently impressed.

XXIX

What though the earlier grooves
170 Which ran the laughing loves
Around thy base, no longer pause and press?
What though, about thy rim,
Skull-things in order grim
Grow out, in graver mood, obey the sterner stress?

151 that **Potter's wheel** *See* Isaiah LXIV:8, and stanzas 82-90 of the *Rubáiyát* 164 **plastic** molding 174 **sterner stress** heavier pressure

XXX

Look not thou down but up!
 To uses of a cup,
The festal board, lamp's flash and trumpet's peal,
  The new wine's foaming flow,
  The Master's lips a-glow!
Thou heaven's consummate cup, what need'st thou with
  earth's wheel?   180

XXXI

But I need, now as then,
 Thee, God, who moldest men;
And since, not even while the whirl was worst,
  Did I,—to the wheel of life
  With shapes and colors rife,
Bound dizzily,—mistake my end, to slake Thy thirst:

XXXII

So, take and use Thy work:
 Amend what flaws may lurk,
What strain o' the stuff, what warpings past the aim!
  My times be in Thy hand!   190
  Perfect the cup as planned!
Let age approve of youth, and death complete the same!

Confessions

I

WHAT is he buzzing in my ears?
 "Now that I come to die,
"Do I view the world as a vale of tears?"
 Ah, reverend sir, not I!

II

What I viewed there once, what I view again
 Where the physic bottles stand
On the table's edge,—is a suburb lane,
 With a wall to my bedside hand.

III

That lane sloped, much as the bottles do,
    From a house you could descry
O'er the garden wall: is the curtain blue
    Or green to a healthy eye?

IV

To mine, it serves for the old June weather
    Blue above lane and wall;
And that farthest bottle labelled "Ether"
    Is the house o'er-topping all.

V

At a terrace, somewhere near the stopper,
    There watched for me, one June,
A girl: I know, sir, it 's improper,
    My poor mind 's out of tune.

VI

Only, there was a way . . . you crept
    Close by the side, to dodge
Eyes in the house, two eyes except:
    They styled their house "The Lodge."

VII

What right had a lounger up their lane?
    But, by creeping very close,
With the good wall's help,—their eyes might strain
    And stretch themselves to Oes,

VIII

Yet never catch her and me together,
    As she left the attic, there,
By the rim of the bottle labelled "Ether,"
    And stole from stair to stair,

IX

And stood by the rose-wreathed gate. Alas,
    We loved, sir—used to meet:
How sad and bad and mad it was—
    But then, how it was sweet!

May and Death

I

I WISH that when you died last May,
  Charles, there had died along with you
Three parts of spring's delightful things;
  Aye, and, for me, the fourth part too.

II

A foolish thought, and worse, perhaps!
  There must be many a pair of friends
Who, arm in arm, deserve the warm
  Moon-births and the long evening-ends.

III

So, for their sake, be May still May!
  Let their new time, as mine of old,   10
Do all it did for me: I bid
  Sweet sights and sounds throng manifold.

IV

Only, one little sight, one plant,
  Woods have in May, that starts up green
Save a sole streak which, so to speak,
  Is spring's blood, spilt its leaves between,—

V

That, they might spare; a certain wood
  Might miss the plant; their loss were small:
But I,—whene'er the leaf grows there,
  Its drop comes from my heart, that 's all.   20

Prospice

FEAR death?—to feel the fog in my throat,
  The mist in my face,
When the snows begin, and the blasts denote
  I am nearing the place,

Title: a Latin motto meaning "Look forward"

The power of the night, the press of the storm,
    The post of the foe;
Where he stands, the Arch Fear in a visible form,
    Yet the strong man must go:
For the journey is done and the summit attained,
    And the barriers fall,
Though a battle 's to fight ere the guerdon be gained,
    The reward of it all.
I was ever a fighter, so—one fight more,
    The best and the last!
I would hate that death bandaged my eyes, and forbore,
    And bade me creep past.
No! let me taste the whole of it, fare like my peers
    The heroes of old,
Bear the brunt, in a minute pay glad life's arrears
    Of pain, darkness and cold.
For sudden the worst turns the best to the brave,
    The black minute 's at end,
And the elements' rage, the fiend voices that rave,
    Shall dwindle, shall blend,
Shall change, shall become first a peace out of pain,
    Then a light, then my breast,
O thou soul of my soul! I shall clasp thee again,
    And with God be the rest!

Youth and Art

I

It once might have been, once only:
    We lodged in a street together,
You, a sparrow on the housetop lonely,
    I, a lone she-bird of his feather.

II

Your trade was with sticks and clay,
    You thumbed, thrust, patted and polished,
Then laughed "They will see some day
    "Smith made, and Gibson demolished."

8 **Gibson** John Gibson (1790-1866), an English sculptor residing in Italy

III

My business was song, song, song;
   I chirped, cheeped, trilled and twittered,   10
"Kate Brown 's on the boards ere long,
   "And Grisi's existence embittered!"

IV

I earned no more by a warble
   Than you by a sketch in plaster;
You wanted a piece of marble,
   I needed a music master.

V

We studied hard in our styles,
   Chipped each at a crust like Hindoos,
For air looked out on the tiles,
   For fun watched each other's windows.   20

VI

You lounged, like a boy of the South,
   Cap and blouse—nay, a bit of beard too;
Or you got it, rubbing your mouth
   With fingers the clay adhered to.

VII

And I—soon managed to find
   Weak points in the flower-fence facing,
Was forced to put up a blind
   And be safe in my corset-lacing.

VIII

No harm! It was not my fault
   If you never turned your eye's tail up,   30
As I shook upon E *in alt,*
   Or ran the chromatic scale up:

IX

For spring bade the sparrows pair,
   And the boys and girls gave guesses,
And stalls in our street looked rare
   With bulrush and watercresses.

12 **Grisi** Giulia Grisi (1811-69), leading operatic soprano of the day
31 **E in alt** high E

X

Why did not you pinch a flower
  In a pellet of clay and fling it?
Why did not I put a power
  Of thanks in a look, or sing it?

40

XI

I did look, sharp as a lynx,
  (And yet the memory rankles)
When models arrived, some minx
  Tripped upstairs, she and her ankles.

XII

But I think I gave you as good!
  "That foreign fellow,—who can know
"How she pays, in a playful mood,
  "For his tuning her that piano?"

XIII

Could you say so, and never say
  "Suppose we join hands and fortunes,
"And I fetch her from over the way,
  "Her, piano, and long tunes and short tunes?"

50

XIV

No, no: you would not be rash,
  Nor I rasher and something over:
You 've to settle yet Gibson's hash,
  And Grisi yet lives in clover.

XV

But you meet the Prince at the Board,
  I 'm queen myself at *bals-paré,*
I 've married a rich old lord,
  And you 're dubbed knight and an R.A.

60

XVI

Each life unfulfilled, you see;
  It hangs still, patchy and scrappy:
We have not sighed deep, laughed free,
  Starved, feasted, despaired,—been happy.

57 **Prince** Albert, the Prince-Consort. **the Board** probably a committee of
the Royal Academy, since the artist is now a member (R. A.) 58 **bals-paré** fancy-dress balls

XVII

And nobody calls you a dunce,
　　And people suppose me clever:
This could but have happened once,
　　And we missed it, lost it forever.

Never the Time and the Place

Never the time and the place
　　And the loved one all together!
This path—how soft to pace!
　　This May—what magic weather!
Where is the loved one's face?
In a dream that loved one's face meets mine,
　　But the house is narrow, the place is bleak
Where, outside, rain and wind combine
　　With a furtive ear, if I strive to speak,
　　With a hostile eye at my flushing cheek,   10
With a malice that marks each word, each sign!
O enemy sly and serpentine,
　　Uncoil thee from the waking man!
　　　　Do I hold the Past
　　　　Thus firm and fast
　　Yet doubt if the Future hold I can?
This path so soft to pace shall lead
Thro' the magic of May to herself indeed!
Or narrow if needs the house must be,
Outside are the storms and strangers: we—   20
Oh, close, safe, warm sleep I and she,
　—I and she!

12 **enemy sly and serpentine** time or change, or the process of life
which blurs memory and shakes faith

Dubiety

I WILL be happy if but for once:
    Only help me, Autumn weather,
Me and my cares to screen, ensconce
    In luxury's sofa-lap of leather!

Sleep? Nay, comfort—with just a cloud
    Suffusing day too clear and bright:
Eve's essence, the single drop allowed
    To sully, like milk, Noon's water-white.

Let gauziness shade, not shroud,—adjust,
    Dim and not deaden,—somehow sheathe
Aught sharp in the rough world's busy thrust,
    If it reach me through dreaming's vapor-wreath.

Be life so, all things ever the same!
    For, what has disarmed the world? Outside,
Quiet and peace: inside, nor blame
    Nor want, nor wish whate'er betide.

What is it like that has happened before?
    A dream? No dream, more real by much.
A vision? But fanciful days of yore
    Brought many: mere musing seems not such.

Perhaps but a memory, after all!
    —Of what came once when a woman leant
To feel for my brow where her kiss might fall.
    Truth ever, truth only the excellent!

Epilogue

At the midnight in the silence of the sleep-time,
   When you set your fancies free,
Will they pass to where—by death, fools think, imprisoned—
Low he lies who once so loved you, whom you loved so,
         —Pity me?

Oh to love so, be so loved, yet so mistaken!
   What had I on earth to do
With the slothful, with the mawkish, the unmanly?
Like the aimless, helpless, hopeless, did I drivel
         —Being—who?   10

One who never turned his back but marched breast forward,
   Never doubted clouds would break,
Never dreamed, though right were worsted, wrong would
    triumph,
Held we fall to rise, are baffled to fight better,
         Sleep to wake.

No, at noonday in the bustle of man's worktime
   Greet the unseen with a cheer!
Bid him forward, breast and back as either should be,
"Strive and thrive!" cry "Speed,—fight on, fare ever
         There as here!"   20

Title: Browning's last poem, published on the day of his death, Dec. 12,
1889, in the volume called *Asolando: Fancies and Facts*

Bibliography

EDITIONS WITH NOTES

The Complete Works of Robert Browning (Florentine Edition). 12 vols, edited with Introduction and Notes by Charlotte Porter and Helen A. Clarke, New York, 1910.

The Works of Robert Browning (Centenary Edition). 10 vols., edited with Introduction by F. G. Kenyon, London, 1912.

The Complete Poetical Works of Robert Browning, New Edition with Additional Poems First Published in 1914, 1 vol., edited by Augustine Birrell, New York, 1915.

The Complete Poetic and Dramatic Works of Robert Browning (Cambridge Edition). 1 vol., Boston, 1895.

BIOGRAPHIES

Orr, Mrs. Sutherland, *Life and Letters of Robert Browning,* London, 1891. (Revised edition by F. G. Kenyon, 1908.)

Griffin, H. W. and Minchin, H. C., *The Life of Robert Browning, With Notices of his Writings, his Family & his Friends,* London, 1910.

Whiting, L., *The Brownings; Their Life and Art,* Boston, 1917.

Chesterton, G. K., *Robert Browning* (English Men of Letters), London, 1903.

Burdett, O., *The Brownings,* Boston, 1929.

BOOKS OF REFERENCE

The Browning Society's Papers, London, 1881-1891.

Cooke, G. W., *A Guide-book to the Poetic and Dramatic Works of Robert Browning,* Boston, 1891.

DeVane, W. C., *A Browning Handbook,* New York, 1935.

CRITICISM

Brooke, Stopford, *The Poetry of Robert Browning,* New York, 1902.

Duckworth, F. G. R., *Browning: Background and Conflicts,* New York, 1932.

Hatcher, H. H., *The Versification of Robert Browning,* Columbus, Ohio, 1928.

Jones, Henry, *Browning as a Philosophical and Religious Thinker,* London, 1891.

Santayana, G., "The Poetry of Barbarism," in *Interpretations of Poetry and Religion,* New York, 1900.

Scott, Dixon, "The Homeliness of Browning" in *Men of Letters,* London, 1916.